Dissuading Terror
Strategic Influence and the Struggle Against Terrorism

Kim Cragin • Scott Gerwehr

T0124843

Approved for public release; distribution unlimited

The research described in this report was supported through the provisions of independent research and development in RAND's contracts for the operation of Department of Defense federally funded research and development centers: RAND Project AIR FORCE (sponsored by the U.S. Air Force), the RAND Arroyo Center (sponsored by the U.S. Army), and the RAND National Defense Research Institute (sponsored by the Office of the Secretary of Defense, the Joint Staff, the unified commands, and the defense agencies).

Library of Congress Cataloging-in-Publication Data

Cragin, Kim.
  Dissuading terror : strategic influence and the struggle against terrorism / Kim Cragin, Scott Gerwehr.
    p. cm.
  "MG-184."
  Includes bibliographical references.
  ISBN 0-8330-3704-8 (pbk. : alk. paper)
  1. Terrorism. 2. Terrorism—United States—Prevention. 3. United States—Strategic aspects. 4. United States—Foreign relations. 5. United States—Influence. I. Gerwehr, Scott, 1968– II. Title.

HV6431.C724 2005
363.32'0973—dc22

2004024269

The RAND Corporation is a nonprofit research organization providing objective analysis and effective solutions that address the challenges facing the public and private sectors around the world. RAND's publications do not necessarily reflect the opinions of its research clients and sponsors.

RAND® is a registered trademark.

Cover design by Stephen Bloodsworth

© Copyright 2005 RAND Corporation

All rights reserved. No part of this book may be reproduced in any form by any electronic or mechanical means (including photocopying, recording, or information storage and retrieval) without permission in writing from RAND.

Published 2005 by the RAND Corporation
1776 Main Street, P.O. Box 2138, Santa Monica, CA 90407-2138
1200 South Hayes Street, Arlington, VA 22202-5050
201 North Craig Street, Suite 202, Pittsburgh, PA 15213-1516
RAND URL: http://www.rand.org/
To order RAND documents or to obtain additional information, contact
Distribution Services: Telephone: (310) 451-7002;
Fax: (310) 451-6915; Email: order@rand.org

Preface

Strategic influence policy—the use of public diplomacy and other information campaigns to promote national security—has come under increased scrutiny since the September 11, 2001, attacks on the World Trade Center and the Pentagon. This scrutiny is due, in part, to new demands in the war on terrorism: The arrest or death of existing terrorists will be only a short-term success if al Qaeda continues to recruit, indoctrinate, and train new members successfully. The U.S. government must therefore determine how it can dissuade new recruits from joining al Qaeda as well as discourage individuals from providing the terrorist organization financial and other support.

This research effort was designed to inform U.S. government decisionmakers about the role that strategic influence policy could play in the struggle against terrorism. It continues a tradition at the RAND Corporation of multidisciplinary research, drawing on academic fields such as social and cognitive psychology as well as terrorism studies.

In the months immediately following the September 11 attacks, RAND undertook several research projects relating to counterterrorism and homeland security topics as elements of its continuing program of self-sponsored research. This report is the result of one of those projects. The work was supported through the provisions for independent research and development in RAND's contracts for the operation of Department of Defense federally funded research and development centers: RAND Project AIR FORCE (sponsored by the U.S. Air Force), the RAND Arroyo Center (sponsored by the U.S.

Army), and the RAND National Defense Research Institute (sponsored by the Office of the Secretary of Defense, the Joint Staff, the unified commands, and the defense agencies). James Chow, Assistant to RAND's President for Research on Counterterrorism, provided overall supervision for this research. Comments on this study are welcomed and should be directed to either the two authors or Dr. Chow.

Contents

Figures

Summary

The U.S. government has long used a strategic influence policy to promote its national security interests. The war on terrorism is no different. Conducting this war effectively requires our government to dissuade terrorists from attacking the United States, divert youths from joining terrorist groups, and persuade the leaders of states and nongovernmental institutions to withhold support for terrorists. This report addresses the role of strategic influence—its potential uses and limitations—in achieving these objectives.

The Parameters of Strategic Influence

The report begins with the question, "What can strategic influence campaigns hope to achieve?" We conclude from our review of the cognitive and social psychology literatures that campaigns have the potential to affect widespread attitudinal change in populations. In addition, influence efforts have the potential to modify the behavior —short and long term—of audiences. Cognitive and social psychology theory indicates, therefore, that strategic influence operations could contribute to the success of U.S. counterterrorism efforts.

Lessons learned from past U.S. influence operations, however, temper this optimism. Specifically, we draw lessons from three influence campaigns conducted by the U.S. government over the past 50 years:

- In post–World War II Germany, General McClure was responsible for "de-Nazification" efforts, which included control over almost every media outlet in Allied-controlled Germany.
- In Vietnam, the U.S. military utilized psychological operations extensively, from dropping pamphlets over enemy territory to using deserters' testimonies against their peers.
- In Eastern Europe, the U.S. government provided support to indigenous anticommunist movements during the Cold War. Specifically, the Polish Underground printed subversive pamphlets and organized strikes, often using U.S. resources.

From these case studies, we conclude that influence campaigns are highly sensitive to operational environments.[1] Moreover, campaigns that do not take these sensitivities into account not only fail but are counterproductive.

Our analysis of the three case studies led us to the following general guidelines for developing effective influence campaigns as well as their possible application.

Match Operational Objectives, Message, and Delivery to the Audience

This first guideline requires a thorough understanding of the target population, incorporating both demographic data (e.g., age, sex, occupation) and psychographics (e.g., perceptions, interests, relationships). In the initial phases of the Vietnam War, for example, the U.S. government distributed numerous pro-American pamphlets to little or no effect. Local populations ignored the pamphlets' messages primarily because they used inappropriate language and iconography. In contrast, during later phases of the *Chieu Hoi* ("open arms") campaign, U.S. forces used defector testimonials—written and in-person—as part of their operations. The defectors understood the mind-set of the target audience (Vietcong forces), and face-to-face

---

[1] By "operational environments," we mean contextual factors, such as the lack of extensive media networks in, for example, rural Yemen, as well as the cultural factors, such as the hierarchical and independent nature of local Yemeni tribes.

testimonials proved to be a more effective method of delivery than the pamphlets.

Incorporate Feedback Mechanisms into the Campaign

Feedback mechanisms are a key factor in the eventual success of an influence campaign. They also provide policymakers with a means of reducing the risk and uncertainty inherent in persuasion techniques. In post-WWII Germany, General McClure instituted frequent and varied polling, surveys, and face-to-face interviews to measure the effectiveness of his programs. This process allowed him to refine both the messages and methods of persuasion over time.

Metrics presuppose a certain degree of knowledge of the intended audiences, which is difficult to determine at the beginning of an influence campaign. The U.S. government was able to resolve this dilemma in the case of the Polish Underground by relying on indigenous institutions to monitor and, more importantly, interpret the campaigns' progress. Notably, both examples demonstrate how understanding the audience and measuring the outcomes are interactive processes.

Set Realistic Expectations

The persuasive efforts in our case studies were often limited by environmental constraints, poor understanding of the audience, and even time. Of the three studies, the most extensive and successful campaign was General McClure's efforts in post-WWII Germany. But our research suggests that it would be very difficult to duplicate this endeavor, primarily because McClure had the ability to control almost all the information outlets in Allied-controlled Germany. This degree of control—and eventually, the widespread conversion of society—is unlikely in today's information age.

Strategic Influence and the Struggle Against Terrorism

While theory and past experience indicate that strategic influence could aid the struggle against terrorism, its sensitivity to operational environments makes the outcome of influence campaigns in the Muslim world uncertain. For this study, we examined Muslim communities in three countries—Yemen, Germany, and Indonesia—that had been home to Islamic terrorist groups prior to the groups attacking U.S. targets. In each of the following cases, local members of the terrorist groups were recruited by or already affiliated with al Qaeda:

- In Yemen, terrorists planned and conducted a maritime attack against the USS *Cole* in October 2000. In this case, al Qaeda operatives—Yemeni expatriates—recruited local militants to participate in the attack.
- In Germany, members of the "Hamburg cell" helped to orchestrate the September 11, 2001, attacks on the World Trade Center and the Pentagon. Al Qaeda leaders apparently recruited, nurtured, and trained members of the Hamburg cell for this attack.
- In Indonesia, members of Jemaah Islamiyah (JI) killed tourists at a Bali nightclub (2002) and bombed the Marriott in Jakarta (2003). The JI is not an al Qaeda cell, but many members have trained in Arab-Afghani camps and the group has an anti-Western agenda.

Given what we learned from these case studies, what then can strategic influence hope to achieve specifically with regard to al Qaeda and the struggle against terrorism? From our analysis of these case studies, we arrived at three key types of audiences in the struggle against terrorism: *terrorists* who attack the United States, *radical institutions* that nurture the terrorists, and *sympathetic communities* that harbor and support the terrorists.

Within each of these categories, we conclude that a confluence of anti-Americanism, radical Islam, and general support for political violence provides an environment in which terrorists can be nurtured or persuaded to conduct attacks against U.S. targets. More importantly, strategic influence campaigns could help to disrupt this confluence. Doing so has the potential, according to our analysis, to reduce future support for al Qaeda and like-minded terrorists.

New Challenges Ahead

Only a few years after the September 11 attacks, the U.S. government is still struggling with how exactly to wage a war on terrorism. It is doubtful that this report—or any other study—can provide a complete answer to this question. RAND analysts have been studying terrorism and counterterrorism tactics for more than 30 years. These studies include analyses of specific groups, such as Gordan McCormick's work on the Shining Path.[2] They also include strategic analyses for understanding emerging threats, such as the study by Bonnie Cordes et al. in 1985 titled *A Conceptual Framework for Analyzing Terrorist Groups*[3] or Ian Lesser et al.'s *Countering the New Terrorism*[4] in 1999. Yet no one has discovered a "silver bullet" to remove the threat of terrorism.

It is also difficult to imagine that strategic influence could be the solution. Like terrorism, RAND analysts have long evaluated the potential strengths and weaknesses of U.S. military psychological operations. If there is one overarching theme to lessons learned in the past, it is that influence is a complex and difficult process—hardly a silver bullet.

Moreover, risks are associated with even simple persuasive campaigns. Programs designed to strengthen the momentum of an

---

[2] Gordan McCormick, *The Shining Path and the Future of Peru*, Santa Monica, Calif.: RAND Corporation, R-3781-DOS/OSD, 1990; Gordan McCormick, *From the Sierra to the Cities: The Urban Campaign of the Shining Path*, Santa Monica, Calif.: RAND Corporation, R-4150-USDP, 1992.

[3] Bonnie Cordes, Brian Michael Jenkins, Konrad Kellen, Gail V. Bass-Golod, Daniel A. Relles, William F. Sater, Mario L. Juncosa, William Fowler, and Geraldine Petty, *A Conceptual Framework for Analyzing Terrorist Groups*, Santa Monica, Calif.: RAND Corporation, R-3151, 1985.

[4] Ian O. Lesser, Bruce Hoffman, John Arquilla, David F. Ronfeldt, and Michele Zanini, *Countering the New Terrorism*, Santa Monica, Calif.: RAND Corporation, MR-989-AF, 1999.

indigenous, nonviolent movement, for example, could reduce its credibility if discovered. Even successful counterpropaganda efforts that weaken a terrorist group's anti-Americanism could accidentally shift animosity onto an important ally. Accurate performance measures can provide decisionmakers with early warnings for adverse consequences. But it is important to acknowledge that strategic influence efforts—from diplomacy to psychological operations—have some uncertainty.

Yet just because strategic influence is not a silver bullet does not mean it is irrelevant. The U.S. government is already engaged in a number of influence campaigns, such as Radio Sawa, that attempt to deal with growing hostility toward the United States. Thus, the aim of this report is to outline how and in what circumstances influence campaigns can best be applied, particularly with regard to the struggle against terrorism.

Acknowledgments

Several people at RAND were integral to the successful completion of this project, providing information and guidance throughout the research effort. In particular, we extend a special note of thanks to colleagues Stephen Hosmer and Lynn Davis for their insights. A number of individuals in the Muslim world also contributed to the completion of our research; at their request, we have not included their names in this report. The authors are also deeply indebted to our two formal reviewers for their constructive criticism and comments. One of these reviewers was Steven Simon (formerly of the National Security Council, now at RAND); the other reviewer's name and affiliation are withheld at the reviewer's request.

Finally, please note that all omissions or mistakes are the sole responsibility of the authors.

Abbreviations

AAIA	Aden Abyan Islamic Army
CBRN	chemical, biological, radiological, or nuclear weapons
GAM	Free Aceh Movement
ICD	Information Control Division
IDF	Islamic Defenders Front
IJM	Islamic Jihad Movement
IO	information operations
JI	Jemaah Islamiyah
LJ	Lashkar Jihad
NGO	nongovernmental organization
PSYOP	psychological operation

CHAPTER ONE

Introduction

The U.S. government has long used influence campaigns in pursuit of national security objectives. These efforts range from covert support for the anticommunist underground media networks in Eastern Europe during the 1980s to public diplomacy efforts in the Arab-Israeli conflict. Yet the September 11, 2001, attacks on the World Trade Center and Pentagon and the subsequent struggle against terrorism have raised new challenges. The U.S. government must now consider how it can prevent terrorists from attacking the United States, discourage sympathizers from supporting terrorist adversaries, and reduce the number of potential new recruits for terrorist groups.

This report examines the potential uses and limitations of influence campaigns in the struggle against terrorism, particularly with regard to al Qaeda and the Muslim world. As such, our study does not explore debates on the root causes of terrorism, the susceptibility of weak states to terrorist threats, or U.S. foreign policy vis-à-vis the Middle East.[1] Instead, it focuses on the intersection between the following trends: (1) animosity toward the United States, (2) support for radical Islam, and (3) violence as a means of political activism. Taken in isolation, any one of these factors is not a significant threat to U.S. national security. However, the combination of all three lays

---

[1] For more information on these issues as they relate to U.S. counterterrorism policy, see Executive Office of the President, "U.S. Counterterrorism Strategy," White House publication, February 2003.

the foundation for terrorism against the United States, as typified by al Qaeda.

Animosity Toward the United States

In the wake of the September 11 attacks, the Gallup Organization commissioned a series of polls to survey attitudes toward the United States in the Muslim world.[2] In a summary document, the authors presented the following findings:

> At almost every opportunity within the survey, respondents overwhelmingly agree that the United States is aptly described by such negative labels as ruthless, aggressive, conceited, arrogant, easily provoked and biased.[3]

> The people of Islamic nations also believe that Western nations do not respect Arab or Islamic values, do not support Arab causes, and do not exhibit fairness towards Arabs, Muslims, or in particular, the situation in Palestine.[4]

These surveys and other expert commentary on al Qaeda fueled a debate among policymakers and in the academic community on Muslim misperceptions of the United States. After all, the United States stands for freedom and democracy—how could anybody hate those things? Yet at the same time, this public discussion raised the issue of American misperceptions of the Muslim world. In addition to the Gallup study, Zogby International published a survey titled, "What Arabs Think: Values, Beliefs, and Concerns."[5] In it, the author stated that the purpose of the survey was to provide American

---

[2] Frank Newport, ed., *The 2002 Gallup Poll of the Islamic World: Tuesday Briefing*, Princeton, N.J.: The Gallup Organization, February 2002.

[3] Newport (2002, p. 4).

[4] Newport (2002, p. 4).

[5] James J. Zogby, *What Arabs Think: Values, Beliefs, and Concerns*, Washington, D.C.: Zogby International, September 2002.

citizens and policymakers with a deeper understanding of the Arab world. The following excerpts are taken from the Zogby publication:

> …what we learned is that Arabs, not unlike other people all over the world, are focused principally on matters of personal security, fulfillment and satisfaction. What matters most are the things that affect them most directly: the quality and the security of their daily work, their faith and their family.[6]

> …after more than three generations of conflicts, and the betrayal and denial of Palestinian rights, this issue appears to have become a defining one of general Arab concern. It is not a foreign policy issue, since foreign policy issues rank near the bottom of priority concerns. Rather…the situation of the Palestinians appears to have become a personal matter.[7]

It is clear from both the Gallup and Zogby studies that anti-Americanism exists in some Muslim communities around the world. What is less clear is whether this animosity is strong enough to translate into violence against the United States. Exploring this interrelationship is a key objective of our report. Indeed, we are not concerned in this study with reducing general hostility toward the United States, unless this hostility causes individuals to support or join terrorist groups that attack U.S. interests.

Support for Radical Islam

"Islam" connotes a number of different philosophical debates and traditions. The two primary categories of beliefs in Islam are Sunni and Shia. Yet even within Sunni Islam, many philosophical differences exist. For example, Wahhabism—the term used to refer to the philosophical tradition that emerged from the teachings of 18th-century Islamic scholar Muhammad ibn 'Abd al-Wahhab—generally

---

[6] Zogby (2002, p. 2).

[7] Zogby (2002, p. 3).

emphasizes Arabic as the true "language of revelation," the authority of religious leaders in interpreting Islam, and a return to the practices of the early Islamic period.[8] In contrast, scholars from what could be termed as the liberal Sunni tradition advocate a belief system that emphasizes modernization and is very much in line with Western liberalism.[9] These two schools of thought illustrate the diversity in the intellectual world of Islam. The philosophical differences also affect the daily lives of Muslims, though to varying degrees. For example, proponents of Wahhabism emphasize personal piety, which translates into, for example, women wearing the *hijab* covering.[10] Notably, this analysis does not probe the philosophical traditions of Islam but rather turns its attention to the application of these beliefs.

This report focuses on "radical Islam." We define the proponents of radical Islam as those individuals who articulate a pan-Islamic worldview. That is, they view the world more in terms of religious unity (*dar el-Islam*) as opposed to nationalistic loyalty, incorporating African, Middle Eastern, and South and Southeast Asian countries with a Muslim majority.[11] Radical Islam proponents also believe that all Muslims should work toward the implementation of Islamic law (e.g., *sharia*) in these countries. Finally, these individuals support the use of violence to achieve their goals.[12]

---

[8] For more information, see Charles Kurzman, *Liberal Islam*, New York: Oxford University Press, 1998, pp. 3–26, and Gilles Kepel, *Jihad: The Trail of Political Islam*, London: I. B. Tauris, 2002, pp. 48–57, 69–75.

[9] Kurzman (1998, pp. 3–26); Kepel (2002, pp. 48–57, 69–75).

[10] Kurzman (1998, pp. 3–26); Kepel (2002, pp. 48–57, 69–75). See also, Donna Lee Bowen and Evelyn A. Early, eds., *Everyday Life in the Muslim Middle East*, 2nd edition, Bloomington, Ind.: Indiana University Press, 2002.

[11] For more information on this counter-movement in the Muslim world, see Kepel (2002, pp. 25–26).

[12] Of course, the terms "implementation" or "interpretation" of *sharia* have different meanings, for example, in Egypt than they do in Malaysia. Similarly, the specific circumstances in which the use of violence is justified also vary across Islamic scholars. Despite this variation, we chose to adopt the term "radical Islam" for this study because it is allows us to concentrate our analysis on the attitudes and interests of those militant groups in the Muslim world that might be willing to use violence against the United States. The term is therefore

Violence as a Means of Political Activism

Individuals' and groups' use of violence underlies this entire study, especially as it interacts with animosity toward the United States and radical Islam. Specifically, we focus on terrorism. In *Inside Terrorism*, Bruce Hoffman states:

> Terrorism is specifically designed to have far-reaching psycho-logical effects beyond the immediate victim(s) or object of the terrorist attack. It is meant to instill fear within, and thereby intimidate, a wider "target audience" that might include a rival ethnic or religious group, an entire country, a national govern-ment or political party, or public opinion in general.... Through the publicity generated by their violence, terrorists seek to obtain the leverage, influence and power they otherwise lack to effect political change on either a local or an international scale.[13]

In contrast to insurgents or guerrilla organizations, terrorists do not use violence to confront state control over people and territory. The purpose of a terrorist campaign is, therefore, not as much control as it is fear. As a result, terrorist groups concentrate their attacks on civil-ians rather than military or police forces, which are the targets of guerrillas and insurgents. Terrorists also have a narrower popular base than insurgents.[14]

Al Qaeda encompasses both types of militant organizations. The core of al Qaeda consists of operatives who conduct terrorist attacks. Yet members of the wider al Qaeda community fight in local insur-gencies, including Afghanistan, Yemen, Kashmir, Algeria, Indonesia, and the Philippines.[15] In the past, al Qaeda leaders have articulated four primary goals: (1) remove U.S. forces from the Persian Gulf region, (2) inspire a pan-Islamic revolution, (3) support the Palestin-

---

sufficient for a study of the role that strategic influence can play in the struggle against ter-rorism.

[13] Bruce Hoffman, *Inside Terrorism*, New York: Colombia University Press, 1998, p. 44.

[14] See Bard O'Neill, *Terrorism and Insurgency*, Washington, D.C.: Brassey's, 1998.

[15] For more information on al Qaeda, see Anonymous, *Through Our Enemy's Eyes*, Washington, D.C.: Brassey's, 2002.

ian cause, and (4) kill large numbers of Americans. [16] The second objective, at least, requires an insurgent-like appeal to Muslim populations, whereas the other three could be incorporated into a terrorist-like strategy. This observation is relevant to our study: Although we focus on al Qaeda as the primary threat, the group does indeed draw some of its members and support from local insurgencies. Therefore, a successful influence campaign directed at al Qaeda will need to address the organization's "hard-core" terrorists, like-minded insurgents, and wider sympathetic communities.

The potential use of chemical, biological, radiological, or nuclear weapons (CBRN) by these militant groups adds a new dimension to the threat.[17] A CBRN attack could increase the number of casualties as well as the "far-reaching psychological effect" identified above in Hoffman's definition of terrorism. Indeed, CBRN capabilities allow terrorists to move beyond the indirect leverage that they gain from the psychological effects of a typical attack (e.g., suicide bombing) to a direct challenge against the state. In this way, terrorist groups can take on the power of an insurgent group, without the risk. State authorities can hold hostage insurgents' supporters and territory, deterring potential CBRN attacks. But this type of counteraction is difficult to achieve for the more unstructured and dispersed terrorist networks.[18] The CBRN threat illustrates how al Qaeda's hard core might articulate objectives (e.g., a CBRN attack against U.S. interests) that place affiliated insurgencies at risk, demonstrating a divergence of interests. For our discussion of strategic influence, a

---

[16] Peter Bergen, *Holy War, Inc.*, New York: Colombia University Press, 2001, pp. 24–40.

[17] For a brief overview of CBRN terrorism, see Richard Falkenrath et al., *America's Achilles' Heel: Nuclear, Biological, and Chemical Terrorism and Covert Attack*, Cambridge, Mass.: MIT Press, 1998.

[18] In their 2002 RAND report, Paul Davis and Brian Jenkins discuss the difficulties inherent in influencing terrorist group behavior. They argue: "Terrorists are not a single foe, and no simple theory of deterrence can possibly apply to the spectrum that ranges from anti-U.S. or anti-Israeli 'martyrs' to members of American right-wing militias…. For these and other reasons, deterrence of such messianic terrorist leaders is likely to be difficult." For more information, see Paul K. Davis and Brian Michael Jenkins, *Deterrence and Influence in Counterterrorism: A Component in the War on al Qaeda*, Santa Monica, Calif.: RAND Corporation, MR-1619-DARPA, 2002.

divergence between al Qaeda and its affiliates is a key policy issue and, therefore, a recurring theme in this report.

Scope and Methodology

Immediately following the September 11 terrorist attacks, academics and policymakers alike asked the question, "Why do they hate us?" Because many believed that anti-Americanism was the result of basic misperceptions about the United States in the Muslim world, the proposed solution was a series of policies aimed at providing more information on U.S. society and foreign policy.

For example, Radio Sawa broadcasts rock music to Muslim youth, interspersing these music programs with news and brief, pro-American summaries of U.S. foreign policy. The effectiveness of this information campaign on the struggle against terrorism is still questionable. Lacking are metrics and methods to determine whether attitudes are changing and, even if so, whether they are changing in the population relevant to terrorism and anti-American activities. We therefore suggest a different approach to the challenge of terrorism and begin our analysis with the question, "What can strategic influence campaigns hope to achieve?"

We use the term *strategic influence* to identify the entire spectrum of influence campaigns, from highly coercive or enticing efforts (e.g., force or bribes) through to public diplomacy. In general, the purpose of these campaigns is to affect the beliefs, opinions, attitudes, and actions of potential adversaries. Influence campaigns could include efforts to deter terrorists from attacking the United States—e.g., "Do not pick up a gun, or we will hunt you down."[19] Alternatively, these campaigns could also incorporate a long-term, educational approach aimed at communities sympathetic to radical Islam

---

[19] "Bush Hails Capture of Top al-Qaeda Operative," *CNN.com*, May 1, 2003. President Bush commented on the arrest of Whalid ba Attash: "When al Qaeda came and killed Americans, there was only one way to deal with them: That was to hunt them down, find them and bring them to justice."

to demonstrate that Islam and democracy are compatible. The challenge for decisionmakers is to match the appropriate objectives to the correct audience and then design an effective message. By asking the question, "What can U.S. policies hope to achieve?" we are able to outline both the possibilities and limitations of influence campaigns and help decisionmakers address this challenge.

To do this, we begin our analysis with an overview of the theory of persuasion. We draw from the scientific literatures of cognitive and social psychology, as well as the principles and practices of persuasion and indoctrination found in advertising, social marketing, sociology, cultural anthropology, and cultic studies disciplines. We chose these disciplines for two reasons. First, they address how one might alter individuals' or communities' beliefs and behaviors in a variety of environments. And second, the sources and methods in the literatures have been well vetted, through both experimental research and application. Although we highlight our sources in the relevant citations, a more thorough listing of the theoretical literature can be found in the bibliography.

We also examine past influence campaigns conducted by the U.S. government. These case studies demonstrate and clarify how strategic influence theory can and cannot be used in an operational setting. The case studies also provide some insight into the strengths and weaknesses of particular influence methods. Specifically, we explore U.S. psychological operations (PSYOPs)[20] during the *Chieu Hoi* ("open arms") campaign in Vietnam. Chieu Hoi was the longest-running U.S. government-sponsored influence campaign in Vietnam. Among its many tactics, the campaign utilized defector testimonials —in written, recorded, and face-to-face interviews—to dissuade support for and attract defectors from the North Vietnamese Army and Vietcong. A large body of published research exists on Chieu Hoi, including the circumstances surrounding the campaign's successes and failures, which helps present many valuable lessons for the role of strategic influence in the struggle against terrorism.

---

[20] At the strategic level, PSYOPs are synonymous with strategic influence efforts as we are defining them.

In addition, we draw lessons from covert U.S. government support of the Polish underground media in the 1980s. This influence campaign focused on supporting an indigenous anticommunist movement in Poland's urban centers, such as Warsaw, Krakow, and Wroclaw. Recently released studies outline how U.S. intelligence agencies covertly supplied equipment and money to an underground media network that distributed dissident pamphlets, newsletters, and books. Importantly, the U.S. government was able to work through existing structures to bolster indigenous anticommunist movements. We believe that parallels exist between the Polish Underground and many moderate Islamic movements. U.S. counterterrorism policy could, therefore, benefit from lessons learned during the Polish Underground campaign.

Finally, our analysis includes a discussion of American "de-Nazification" efforts in postwar Germany. After World War II, President Eisenhower asked Brigadier General Robert McClure, head of U.S. Psychological Warfare Division during the war, to oversee the Information Control Division (ICD) in occupied postwar Germany. McClure's influence campaign was extensive. One expert stated, "Their effort must be ranked as one of the single largest campaigns of purposive communication ever undertaken by a democratic society."[21] Some policymakers have suggested that today's reconstruction efforts in Iraq could have an effect similar to those in post-WWII Germany.[22] Thus, we determine that an analysis of the scope of this influence campaign could prove useful to U.S. decisionmakers.

Having begun with the question, "What can influence hope to achieve?" we next explore the application of strategic influence in the struggle against terrorism. Doing so requires a thorough understanding of our potential audiences. This report examines three countries with Muslim populations that have articulated animosity toward the United States, have supported radical Islamic agendas, and have

---

[21] Christopher Simpson, *Science of Coercion: Communication Research and Psychological Warfare 1945–1960*, New York: Oxford University Press, 1994.

[22] President Bush alluded to this in his speech before the American Enterprise Institute. Office of the Press Secretary, "President Discusses the Future of Iraq," February 26, 2003.

members who have conducted attacks against U.S. interests. They are Yemen, Germany, and Indonesia.

In our analysis of Yemen, we examine the intersection between sources of animosity toward the United States, patterns of support for radical Islam, and political violence. To do this, we focus on the manifestation of these trends in the al Qaeda cell responsible for the October 12, 2000, attack on the USS *Cole*. We also assess the same interaction with regard to the Moroccan diaspora in Germany and its representation in the "Hamburg cell" that participated in the September 11 attacks. Finally, we include an analysis of the terrorists who supported and perpetrated the October 12, 2002, attacks in Bali.

We chose these three countries because they represent a wide range of cultures, societal structures, and exposure to the United States. In addition, they produced terrorists who have conducted some of the most virulently anti-Western attacks of the past few years. Research on these three countries is drawn from news reports; historical, sociological, and religious studies; and expert interviews.

Notably, we do not purport to take lessons learned from past strategic influence experiences and apply them directly to ongoing U.S. strategic influence campaigns. The methodology of lessons learned is such that it can only produce guidelines for decisionmakers to consider in designing U.S. policy. Moreover, we do attempt to generalize our findings for Yemen, Germany, or Indonesia across the entire Muslim world. In examining these three Muslim communities, our aim is to help contextualize general principles of strategic influence and relate them to a post–September 11 world. Our observations should, therefore, be viewed as potential guidelines for refining U.S. strategic influence as it relates to the struggle against terrorism. We conclude this report by presenting our findings in the context of U.S. national security policy.

Report Structure

The chapters in this report are organized along the lines of the methodology used. The following chapter, Chapter Two, includes a discussion of strategic influence theory, incorporating social and cognitive psychology literatures as well as other disciplines involving persuasion and indoctrination. Chapter Three explores what strategic influence can hope to achieve—its uses and limitations—using lessons drawn from past U.S. strategic influence campaigns. This chapter concludes by proposing ways of evaluating the effectiveness of influence operations and the dangers of failure. Chapter Four turns to a discussion of radical Islam, political violence, and animosity toward the United States in the Muslim world. This chapter includes our analysis of Yemen, Indonesia, and the Moroccan diaspora in Germany. We then explore, in Chapter Five, the role of strategic influence in the struggle against terrorism, concluding with brief observations on potential challenges ahead.

CHAPTER TWO

The Theoretical Underpinnings of Strategic Influence

> Four hostile newspapers are more to be feared than a thousand bayonets.
>
> —*Napoleon Bonaparte*[1]

The assumption behind strategic influence is that a persuasive campaign—e.g., utilizing media or other forms of information operations—can help advance national interests. Following the September 11, 2001, attacks, the U.S. government identified terrorism as a key national security issue.[2] For this reason, strategic influence has a role to play in the struggle against terrorism, by attempting to shape the actions of existing and potential terrorist adversaries. This chapter explores the theoretical underpinnings of strategic influence to better understand both its uses and its limitations.

To do this, we draw on experimental research in the scientific literatures of social and cognitive psychology, as well as disciplines rooted in persuasion and indoctrination. Notably, the concepts included in this chapter are by no means new. Academics and policymakers alike have studied influence for nearly a century, attempting

---

[1] In *Maxims of War* (compiled by General Burnod), 1827 (copyright expired).

[2] For more information, see the Executive Office of the President (2003).

to apply the theories in wartime as well as peacetime.[3] In this report, we have simply consolidated these theories to better assess their potential in the struggle against terrorism.[4] We define *influence campaigns* as follows:

> An influence campaign uses planned operations—covert and/or overt—to convey selected information and indicators to foreign audiences. Such campaigns attempt to influence the perceptions, cognitions, and behavior of foreign governments, organizations, groups, and individuals. The purpose of psychological operations is to induce or reinforce foreign behavior favorable to the originator's overall political and strategic objectives.[5]

By adopting the term *strategic influence,* we attempt to go beyond the means and methods of a particular influence operation. Instead, we propose that influence campaigns have strategic implications for U.S. national security policy.

The Psychological Objectives of Persuasion

Influence campaigns can produce a variety of real-world behaviors. For example, a campaign might stimulate a workers' strike, galvanize a large number of people to migrate across borders, or even modify a social habit (e.g., smoking) on a large scale. But before an operation can produce these behaviors, it must first alter the target audiences' attitudes, opinions, reasoning, and/or emotions. The term "psychological objectives" identifies the ways in which policymakers might want to affect audiences' outlook.

---

[3] See, for example, George Creel, *How We Advertised America*, New York: Arno Press, 1972, or Walter Lippman, *Public Opinion*, New York: Harcourt-Brace, 1922.

[4] Note that we discuss only some of the many models relevant to influence theory. A survey of the literature is beyond the scope of this report; however, we have included additional reference works in our bibliography.

[5] This is an adaptation of the definition for psychological operations found in U.S. Joint Chiefs of Staff, *Joint Doctrine for Psychological Operations,* Joint Publication 3-53, 1996.

Figure 2.1 illustrates how psychological objectives are best understood as a spectrum of effects. Along this spectrum, three distinct milestones exist: compliance, conformity, and conversion (discussed below). Influence theory suggests that one factor in the success or failure of a persuasion operation is whether or not policymakers match the appropriate psychological objective with the desired behavior.[6]

Compliance

In simple terms, the theme of a compliance campaign is, "Believe what you want, but do what we say." For example, a political candidate who pays university students to attend a rally is conducting a compliance-type influence campaign. The candidate is not changing the students' beliefs or attitudes[7] in the short, medium, or long term,

Figure 2.1
The Spectrum of Psychological Objectives

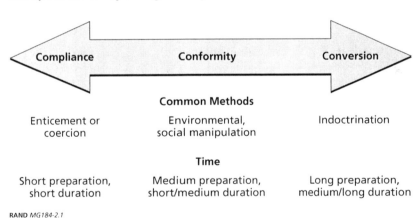

Compliance	Conformity	Conversion

Common Methods

Enticement or coercion	Environmental, social manipulation	Indoctrination

Time

Short preparation, short duration	Medium preparation, short/medium duration	Long preparation, medium/long duration

RAND MG184-2.1

---

[6] See, for example, S. Chaiken and A. Eagly, "Communication Modality as a Determinant of Message Persuasiveness and Message Comprehensibility," *Journal of Personality and Social Psychology*, No. 34, 1976.

[7] A belief is an opinion or set of related opinions (e.g., "I support environmental conservation"), while an attitude is an opinion about a particular object or idea (e.g., "Littering is a bad thing").

but rather is causing an immediate change in their behavior. Essentially, the candidate is purchasing a certain type of behavior, regardless of what the students believe. Indeed, bribery, in various forms, is a tool often used to elicit compliance. Force or the threat of force is the other tool used in compliance campaigns.[8]

An effective compliance operation has three main characteristics: (1) sufficient inducement, (2) few or no obstacles to obedience, and (3) a simple set of instructions for the audience to follow.[9] If these three elements are present, the desired behaviors usually ensue.[10] Compliance campaigns have a benefit in that the audiences' response is often visible and immediate. Similarly, these campaigns—e.g., using force or bribery—typically require only a short amount of time to implement, which can also be advantageous to the policymaker.

Although a compliance operation can gain an immediate response in audiences, it has some limitations. The scientific literature of attitude change (dissonance theory) suggests strongly that, in these circumstances, the audiences' beliefs do not change.[11] Because the attribution for the anomalous behavior can be laid at the feet of the exogenous source (e.g., "I only did it because there was a gun to my head"), dissonance theory suggests that the receivers' attitudes are less likely to change in a way that is favorable to the sender.[12] What this limitation means for policymakers is that compliance-type campaigns have a tendency to last only a short amount of time, usually not beyond the presence of the inducing stimulus.[13]

---

[8] Stephen T. Hosmer, *Psychological Effects of U.S. Air Operations in Four Wars 1941–1991: Lessons for U.S. Commanders*, Santa Monica, Calif.: RAND Corporation, MR-576-AF, 1996.

[9] S. Milgram, *Obedience to Authority*, New York: Harper & Row, 1974; S. Milgram, *Obedience to Authority: An Experimental View*, New York: Harper-Collins, 1983.

[10] Milgram (1974); Milgram (1983).

[11] See L. Festinger, *A Theory of Cognitive Dissonance*, Stanford, Calif.: Stanford University Press, 1957, and L. Festinger and J. M. Carlsmith, "Cognitive Consequences of Forced Compliance," *Journal of Abnormal and Social Psychology*, No. 58, 1959.

[12] Festinger (1957); Festinger and Carlsmith (1959).

[13] Festinger and Carlsmith (1959); E. Schein, *Coercive Persuasion*, New York: Norton, 1961; Milgram (1983).

Conformity

Conformity has been well studied—from adolescent peer pressure to wartime combatants' behavior—and is a complex issue.[14] Conformational pressures arise from contextual or environmental cues that trigger individuals to behave in a manner that seems appropriate or correct, given the situation.[15] If compliance can be summarized as, "Believe what you want, but do what we say," then conformity is, "Do what your context suggests is appropriate or correct." The influence campaign is designed to define appropriateness and correctness.

We divide conformational persuasion into *normative* social influence and *informational* social influence. For normative social influence, individuals compare their behavior with similar individuals around them, modeling their own behavior after their peers to gain social validation.[16] A number of factors can affect the success or failure of a campaign that seeks to persuade audiences through the use of normative social influence. For example, research demonstrates that the greater the unanimity of the peer group, the greater the influence on an individual's behavior.[17] Other factors include the presence or absence of counterarguments and time constraints on the audiences' decisionmaking processes.[18] The presence of counterarguments can

---

[14] S. E. Asch "Effects of Group Pressure upon the Modification and Distortion of Judgment," in H. Guetzkow, ed., *Groups, Leadership, and Men*, Pittsburgh, Pa.: Carnegie Press, 1951; C. Insko, R. Smith, M. Alicke, J. Wade, and S. Taylor, "Conformity and Group Size: The Concern with Being Right and the Concern with Being Liked," *Personality and Social Psychology*, No. 11, 1985; M. Sakarai, "Small Group Cohesiveness and Detrimental Conformity," *Sociometry*, No. 38, 1975; C. Maslach, J. Stapp, and R. Santee, "Individuation," *Journal of Personality and Social Psychology*, No. 49, 1985.

[15] Asch (1951); C. Insko et al. (1985); Sakarai (1975); Maslach, Stapp, and Santee (1985).

[16] M. Deutch and H. B. Gerard, "A Study of Normative and Informational Social Influence upon Judgement," *Journal of Abnormal and Social Psychology*, No. 51, 1955.

[17] Asch (1951); S. E. Asch "Studies of Independence and Conformity: A Minority of One Against a Unanimous Majority," *Psychological Monographs*, Vol. 70, No. 416, 1956; Irving Janis, *Groupthink: Psychological Studies of Policy Decisions and Fiascos*, 2nd edition, Boston: Houghton Mifflin, 1982.

[18] Deutch and Gerard (1955); W. J. McGuire "Inducing Resistance to Persuasion," in L. Berkowitz, ed., *Advances in Experimental Social Psychology*, Vol. 1, New York: McGraw-Hill, 1964, pp. 192–229; S. Moscovici, "Social Influence and Conformity," in G. Lindzey and E. Aronson, eds., *Handbook of Social Psychology*, Vol. 2, New York: McGraw-Hill, 1985;

bolster an individual's resistance to normative social influence; so can a significant amount of time the individual might have to process and digest the influence attempt.

In the case of informational social influence, individuals cue off facts or information (e.g., news) and adjust their behavior accordingly. This type of psychological objective is a common form of persuasion in Western cultures, where media consumption is high and cultural norms exist for decisionmaking based on that consumption.[19] As with normative social influence, a number of variables affect the success or failure of an informational campaign. These variables include the presence or absence of relevant facts, the credibility of the communicator, and the format of the message.[20]

Conformity-type campaigns are less direct than those of compliance, manipulating the context instead of the individual. As a result, these campaigns usually require more time to affect the audience than compliance-type efforts.[21] Scientific research and experience have shown, however, that conformational pressure can produce some

---

Irving Janis, *Victims of Groupthink*, Boston: Houghton Mifflin, 1972; P. Tetlock, R. Peterson, C. Mcguire, S. Chang, and P. Feld, "Assessing Political Group Dynamics: A Test of the Groupthink Model," *Journal of Personality and Social Psychology*, Vol. 63, No. 3, 1992.

[19] See, for example, D. Schumann, R. Petty, and D. Clemons, "Predicting the Effectiveness of Different Strategies of Advertising Variation," *Journal of Consumer Research*, No. 17, 1990.

[20] C. Hovland and W. Weiss, "The Influence of Source Credibility on Communication Effectiveness," *Public Opinion Quarterly*, No. 15, 1951; A. Eagly, W. Wood, and S. Chaiken, "Causal Inferences About Communicators and Their Effect on Opinion Change," *Journal of Personality and Social Psychology*, No. 36, 1978; C. Lord, L. Ross, and M. Lepper, "Biased Assimilation and Attitude Polarization," *Journal of Personality and Social Psychology*, No. 37, 1979; H. Schuman and S. Presser, "Questions and Answers in Attitude Surveys: Experiments on Question Form, Wording and Context," Orlando, Fla.: Academic Press, 1981.

[21] Moscovici (1985); A. Andreasen, *Marketing Social Change: Changing Behavior to Promote Health, Social Development, and the Environment*, San Francisco: Jossey-Bass, 1995; Carl I. Hovland, Irving Janis, and Harold Kelley, "Communication and Persuasion: Psychological Studies in Opinion Change," New Haven, Conn.: Yale University Press, 1953; M. Fishbein, M. Goldberg, and S. Middlestadt, Social Marketing: *Theoretical and Practical Perspectives*, Atlanta, Ga.: Erlbaum, 1997.

change in attitudes—as well as desired behaviors—and thus can have a more enduring impact than compliance efforts.[22]

Conversion

As the term implies, conversion entails the complete restructuring of the audiences' relevant beliefs, attitudes, emotions, and opinions.[23] Desired behaviors eventually emerge without prompting, once the attitudes that underlie them have changed. For example, converting a member of Party X to Party Y should generally lead the individual to vote for Y-type candidates; further inducement is not critical. A conversion campaign might, therefore, be summarized as, "Believe what we say, then behave accordingly."

In the most effective conversion-type campaigns, policymakers have significant control over the environment in which the audience lives and operates.[24] This control allows policymakers to overcome the challenge of counter-conversion attempts by adversaries. Research also demonstrates that the most effective conversion efforts come from trusted, credible, knowledgeable sources similar or related to the target.[25] Conversion-type campaigns can be difficult to implement;

---

[22] J. Rohrer, S. Baron, E. Hoffman, and D. Swander, "The Stability of Autokinetic Judgments," *Journal of Abnormal and Social Psychology*, No. 49, 1954; J. Campbell, A. Tesser, and P. Fairey, "Conformity and Attention to the Stimulus: Temporal and Contextual Dynamics," *Journal of Personality and Social Psychology*, No. 51, 1986.

[23] This restructuring is also referred to as the "internalization" of attitude change. For more information, see P. Zimbardo and M. Leippe, *The Psychology of Attitude Change and Social Influence*, Boston: McGraw-Hill, 1991.

[24] For more information, see Robert J. Lifton, *Thought Reform and the Psychology of Totalism*, New York: Norton, 1969.

[25] I. Altman and D. Taylor, "Communication in Interpersonal Relationships: Social Penetration Theory," in M. E. Roloff and G. R. Miller, eds., *Interpersonal Processes: New Directions in Communication Research*, Newbury Park, Calif.: Sage, 1987; H. Giles and J. M. Wiemann "Language, Social Comparison and Power," in C. R. Berger and S. H. Chafee, eds., *The Handbook of Communication Science*, Newbury Park, Calif.: Sage, 1987; Hovland and Weiss (1951).

they are also resource intensive and generally take the longest amount of time to prepare and execute.[26]

Observations

Importantly, the methods of persuasion that suit one type of objective may be inappropriate—or even counterproductive—for accomplishing another. For example, a coercive campaign that utilizes force might gain immediate compliance but would not be appropriate for longer-term conversion attempts. This challenge is particularly difficult when compliance and conversion campaigns run in parallel. A *New York Times* article reported Lieutenant General Ricardo Sanchez's comments on this challenge in the context of postwar Iraq in August 2003:

> [The Iraqi] message, [Sanchez] said, has been that "when you take a father in front of his family and put a bag over his head and put him on the ground, you have a significant adverse effect on his dignity and respect in the eyes of his family." General Sanchez said the message from the Iraqis was that in doing this, you create more enemies than you capture.[27]

This difficulty is clear in the context of U.S. policy in Iraq, in which it is easy to see how security-related objectives (e.g., locating key Iraqi dissidents) could easily interfere with reconstruction objectives (e.g., creating goodwill toward U.S. forces among Iraqi civilians). Yet similar challenges can arise even within less-constrained policy circumstances. For example, the polling discussed in Chapter One of this report suggests that U.S. foreign policy objectives with regard to the Palestinian issue might reduce the credibility of the U.S. government in other parts of the Muslim world and therefore pose a chal-

---

[26] R. E. Petty and J. T. Cacioppo, *Communication and Persuasion: Central and Peripheral Routes to Attitude Change*, New York: Springer-Verlag, 1986; A. Bandura, *Principles of Behavior Modification*, New York: Holt, Rinehart and Winston, 1969; A. Eagly and S. Chaiken, *The Psychology of Attitudes*, Fort Worth, Tex.: Harcourt Brace Jovanovich, 1993.

[27] "To Mollify Iraqis, US Plans to Ease Scope of Its Raids," *New York Times*, August 7, 2003.

lenge to influence campaigns in the struggle against terrorism. In many cases, these challenges cannot be resolved or eliminated simply through better planning; trade-offs are necessary. Understanding the extent of the challenge, however, can help policymakers discern the potential uses and limitations of influence operations.

The Necessary Sequence of Events and Timing

Issues of sequencing and timing are also integral to persuasion. The term *sequence* identifies the series of events required to translate influence into desired action, as illustrated by Figure 2.2. *Timing* is the duration of these series of events. The figure is drawn from a theoretical approach to the concept of influence that was developed over decades of scientific research—often referred to as the Yale model of persuasion.[28] It illustrates the six stages that any influence attempt—compliance through conversion—must go through in order to be effective. At this point, we should note that the Yale model is only one of several theoretical models of persuasive communication. Others include the Elaboration Likelihood Model by Richard Petty and John Cacioppo[29] and the Heuristic-Systematic Model by Alice Eagly and Shelly Chaiken[30]. We chose to use the Yale model because

---

[28] For more information, see Hovland, Janis, and Kelley (1953); M. Sherif and C. L. Hovland, *Social Judgment: Assimilation and Contrast Effects in Communication and Attitude Change,* New Haven, Conn.: Yale University Press, 1961; McGuire (1964); and W. J. McGuire, "Personality and Susceptibility to Social Influence," in E. Borgatta and W. Lambert, eds., *Handbook in Personality Theory and Research*, Chicago: Rand McNally, 1968.

[29] R. Petty and J. Cacioppo, *Attitudes and Persuasion: Classic and Contemporary Approaches*, Dubuque, Iowa: Wm. C. Brown, 1981; Petty and Cacioppo (1986).

[30] S. Chaiken, "The Heuristic Model of Persuasion," in M. P. Zanna, J. M. Olson, and C. P. Herman, eds., *Social Influence: The Ontario Symposium*, Hillsdale, N.J.: Erlbaum, 1987; S. Chaiken, A. Liberman, and A. H. Eagly, "Heuristic and Systematic Information Processing Within and Beyond the Persuasion Context," in J. S. Uleman and J. A. Bargh, eds., *Unintended Thought*, New York: Guilford Press, 1989; Eagly and Chaiken (1993).

Figure 2.2
Sequence of Events in Persuasive Communication

RAND *MG184-2.2*

it is well regarded among experts of influence theory and because it illustrates the complexity of the challenge. This choice does not, however, invalidate the other models.

Exposure. The first stage required to translate influence into desired action is exposure.[31] In general, exposure requires that the message reach the audience; for example, an elaborate radio campaign is ineffective if the target audience does not listen to the station used to transmit.[32] To achieve their psychological objectives, policymakers must transmit the persuasive message through a *correct* channel to the *appropriate* audience (by which we mean the audience that can directly or indirectly produce the desired response).

Attention. Even if the message is transmitted through the correct channels, the appropriate audience still might not notice it. Attention can sometimes be difficult to achieve. The world is a noisy place: New messages compete with contradictory information and sheer background noise, which can drown out any persuasive communication.[33] The message should be crafted to pierce this surrounding noise.

---

[31] See, for example, K. Short, ed., "Broadcasting Over the Iron Curtain," New York: St. Martin's, 1986; L. Soley, *Radio Warfare: OSS and CIA Subversive Propaganda,* Westport, Conn.: Praeger, 1989; A. R. Johnson "Winning Hearts and Minds: Cold War Victories and Post 9/11 Challenges," *Hoover Digest,* Fall 2003.

[32] This observation holds true both for countries in which media is widespread (the message should be transmitted over the correct channel) and for those in which they are less widespread (adopting a media campaign can be less than effective if individuals do not have access to radios, televisions, or newspapers).

[33] For more information, see Aimee Drolet and Jennifer Aaker, "Off-Target? Changing Cognitive-Based Attitudes," *Journal of Consumer Research,* Vol. 12, No. 1, 2002.

Comprehension. An influence campaign must ensure that the intended audience understands the persuasive communication. Comprehension requires policymakers to craft and deliver the message in a culturally appropriate manner, employing syntax, images, words, concepts, and intentions that are tailored to the audience. Notably, a linguistically or idiomatically ill-suited message will likely fail and could be counterproductive.[34]

Acceptance. The target audience must not only comprehend the message but accept it. Indeed, a well-crafted message can be transmitted, noticed, and comprehended but still trigger instant rejection by audiences if it is not formatted to gain their acceptance.[35] One example of how this rejection occurs is the inappropriate use of *schemas*, cognitive shortcuts that reduce the burden of deep thinking and quicken reactions. Schemas can have great utility—quickly associating smoke with fire has survival value—but they can also be problematic. For example, the use of the term "crusade" is likely to invoke a negative schema among Muslims around the world, recalling Christian forces colonizing Muslim lands in the name of religion hundreds of years ago. For this reason, a U.S. radio broadcast wherein President Bush refers to the struggle against terrorism as a crusade is likely to invoke a negative schema among Muslim audiences.[36] In these situations, this one word could cause listeners to "tune out" or reject entire—and possibly even future—messages.[37]

---

[34] A. Eagly, "Comprehensibility of Persuasive Arguments as a Determinant of Opinion Change," *Journal of Personality and Social Psychology*, No. 29, 1974, pp. 758–773.

[35] Chaiken (1987); Chaiken, Liberman, and Eagly (1989); Petty and Cacioppo (1986).

[36] Immediately after the September 11 attacks, President Bush used the word "crusade" in describing the campaign against al Qaeda and terrorism. For information on how the international community responded, see David Wastell, "Bush Speech Crafted to Unify Hawks and Doves in Cabinet," *Telegraph.co.uk,* September 23, 2001, and Peter Ford, "Europe Cringes at President Bush's 'Crusade' Against Terrorism," *Christian Science Monitor,* September 19, 2001.

[37] R. Hass, "Effects of Source Characteristics on Cognitive Response and Persuasion" in R. E. Petty, T. M. Ostrom, and T. C. Brock, eds., *Cognitive Responses in Persuasion,* Hillsdale, N.J.: Erlbaum, 1981.

Retention. Even an influential message must have a "durable" effect on the target audiences—meaning that the audience remembers the persuasive message long enough for the desired behavior to emerge at a propitious time.[38] In the context of terrorism, a propitious time could be the moment a son asks his family for their blessing in joining an extremist group, the moment a pedestrian sees a leaflet advertising a recruitment event and is deciding whether to attend, or any other crucial juncture in the life cycle of terrorism. Notably, the retention requirements of an influence operation depend on the operation's objectives. A few minutes may be long enough to galvanize the surrender of terrorists in a cave, but a few years may be needed to reduce an organization's monetary support.

Translation. Translation entails cognitive change leading to behavioral change, or the translation of perception into action. For translation to occur, an unobstructed path must exist for changes in an individual's attitude to result in changes in his or her behavior.[39] For example, the target audience may truly experience a change in attitude, yet be restrained by repressive societies or authoritative leaders. The literature on social psychology indicates that circumstances strongly influence actual decisionmaking.[40] Thus, influence programs have a greater possibility of success if they are conducted in an environment that facilitates the translation of changes in attitude into behavior.

Observations

The sequence of events above represents the steps that an influence campaign must navigate to be successful. This sequence might take

---

[38] C. I. Hovland, A. Lumsdaine, and F. Sheffield, *Experiments on Mass Communication*, Princeton, N.J.: Princeton University Press, 1949; Hovland and Weiss (1951).

[39] See, for example, J. M. Darley and C. D. Batson, "From Jerusalem to Jericho: A Study of Situational and Dispositional Variables in Helping Behavior," *Journal of Personality and Social Psychology*, No. 27, 1973.

[40] For more information on how the environment affects decisionmaking, see Asch (1951); Harold Lasswell, "The Structure and Function of Communication in Society," in Lyman Bryson, ed., *The Communication of Ideas*, New York: Harper & Row, 1948; Janis (1982); and Petty and Cacioppo (1986).

less time, for example, for a conformity campaign than for a conversion campaign, but the sequence itself remains constant. The theories behind strategic influence indicate that a successful campaign goes beyond "sending a powerful message." Indeed, *sending* a message is only the beginning of persuasion, especially in cross-cultural settings.

Key Judgments

Persuasion theory holds a number of key insights for the use and limitations of influence operations. Significantly, misconstruing the ultimate psychological objectives of an influence campaign or not matching these objectives appropriately to audiences can decrease the effectiveness of a campaign. The theory of persuasion also suggests that a more effective operation accounts for sequencing and timing requirements. The theoretical underpinnings of persuasion, therefore, challenge policymakers to determine both how influence fits within the government's overall goals and what methods to employ.

Next, we explore influence operations conducted by the U.S. government in the past and methods of evaluating the effectiveness of such campaigns. The persuasion theory, presented above, helps us make sense of these case studies and allows us to clarify the potential uses and limitations of strategic influence.

CHAPTER THREE

Theory into Practice:
What Influence Can Hope to Achieve

Although the theory of persuasion provides parameters for the use of influence campaigns, it is difficult to conceptualize these parameters in the day-to-day existence of U.S. national security policy. The purpose of this chapter is to help alleviate this difficulty. To do this, we provide a short overview of past influence campaigns, including discussions of the methods used as well as lessons learned from U.S. efforts in post–World War II Germany, Vietnam, and Poland. We next examine performance measures, which can help policymakers determine the effectiveness of an influence campaign. Finally, we conclude with a discussion of the limitations of influence campaigns, emphasizing the potentially negative consequences of an ill-thought-out or unsuccessful campaign.

Instruments and Methods of Influence

The most common instruments of persuasion are various forms of media, including radio, television, movies, and newspapers. Such instruments have been developed and applied by U.S. policymakers during times of war and peace. The following sections outline some of the instruments and methods used in past influence campaigns, specifically in post-WWII Germany, Vietnam, and Poland. The purpose of this discussion is not to provide an exhaustive list of persuasion operations, but rather to distill key lessons.

Germany, Post–World War II

As the fighting in the European theater approached its culmination in 1945, the Allies began to plan for the physical reconstruction of Germany. The Allies identified the "de-Nazification" of postwar Germany as one of their key tasks, determining that it should run in parallel with the Marshall Plan.[1] U.S. President Eisenhower selected Brigadier General Robert Alexis McClure, head of the Psychological Warfare Division of the U.S. Army during the war, to accomplish this task. Assuming leadership of the newly created Information Control Division, General McClure took responsibility for designing an influence campaign that would reshape the militarism and ethnocentrism seen to be at the root of German warfare.[2] General McClure and the ICD implemented expansive conformity- and conversion-type operations, which included the following methods of influence:

- development, publication, and distribution of the *Stars & Stripes* daily newspaper
- implementation of specially designed education programs for German military personnel
- production and distribution of 50 to 75 documentary films per year as well as daily newsreels released in cinemas
- control over postal censorship, which included the licensing of all newspaper, magazine, and book publishers
- creation of new cultural centers in 60 German cities.

We draw two key lessons from this case study that have direct relevance to the role of persuasion in the struggle against terrorism.

First, the instruments of persuasion can be difficult and costly to manage. General McClure began his task by shutting down every

---

[1] W. Ziemke, *The US Army in the Occupation of Germany 1944–1946*, Washington, D.C.: Center of Military History, 1975; Jeffrey Diefendorf, Axel Frohn, and Hermann Rupieper, eds., *American Policy and the Reconstruction of West Germany, 1945–1955*, New York: Cambridge University Press, 1993; Simpson (1994).

[2] Edgar McInnis, Richard Hiscocks, and Robert Spencer, "The Shaping of Postwar Germany," New York: Praeger, 1960.

indigenous media source in the areas of Germany under Allied control.[3] The ICD then filled this information void with its own media campaigns, which were antimilitarist, anti-Nazi, and pro-Allied. The language and details of these messages varied according to target audiences, but each message was integrated into the broader "de-Nazify" agenda.[4] Evaluations of General McClure's efforts demonstrate that the ICD campaign was successful, but an important factor in this success was the ability of the ICD to dominate the media networks.[5] This degree of control is almost unimaginable in today's information age. Moreover, General McClure's influence campaign was expensive, measuring in the hundreds of millions of today's dollars in addition to the cost of the physical reconstruction of Germany.[6] Relatively speaking, the audiences in post-WWII Germany were small and uniform compared with the audiences that the U.S. government faces today in the struggle against terrorism. This case study therefore indicates that successful conversion- and conformity-type campaigns can be costly—if often overlooked—components of U.S. national security strategy.

Second, it is important to measure the effectiveness of influence instruments frequently. General McClure incorporated multiple forms of metrics into the ICD's campaigns that were aimed at identifying and measuring changes in German attitudes. These metrics included surveys, focus groups, and face-to-face interviews across the range of German demographics and psychographics.[7] The responses from these surveys allowed the ICD to adjust its methods to improve the operations' overall results. For example, ICD surveys determined that certain newspapers were effective at "maintaining and deepening

---

[3] Simpson (1994); Thomas A. Schwartz, *America's Germany*, Cambridge, Mass.: Harvard University Press, 1991.

[4] Ziemke (1975); McInnis (1960); Schwartz (1991).

[5] Simpson (1994).

[6] Simpson (1994); Ziemke (1975).

[7] Demographics include information, for example, on the age, sex, or occupation of potential audiences, whereas psychographic intelligence incorporates additional data on perceptions, interests, and opinions.

the mood of passive acquiescence to the Allied occupation."[8] In response, the ICD arranged subsidies, tax exemptions, low rents, and a steady supply of raw materials for those newspapers to ensure their existence and expansion.[9] Indeed, the ICD eventually refined every aspect of the influence campaign, from the production of materials to their dissemination.[10] The U.S. government faces similar challenges in the struggle against terrorism, making it logical to incorporate performance measures, especially in regions where the United States is fighting to overcome the influence of al Qaeda and like-minded terrorist groups.

Vietnam, 1963–1972

Nearly 20 years after World War II, the U.S. government conducted the *Chieu Hoi* ("open arms") campaign in coordination with its military operations in Vietnam.[11] This campaign had multiple psychological objectives—from compliance to conversion—against adversaries in Vietnam.[12] U.S. forces directed these efforts against North Vietnamese Army regulars, Vietcong guerrillas, U.S.-sponsored Vietnamese forces (GVN [Government of Vietnam] and ARVN [Army of the Republic of Vietnam]), and Vietnamese noncombatants with mixed results. The very extent of the Chieu Hoi campaign, and its

---

[8] Ziemke (1975).

[9] Ziemke (1975).

[10] R. Chandler, *War of Ideas: The U.S. Propaganda Campaign in Vietnam*, Boulder, Colo.: Westview, 1981; C. Page, *U.S. Official Propaganda During the Vietnam War: 1965–1973*, London: Leicester University Press, 1996.

[11] Excellent and extensive scholarship exists on U.S. influence efforts undertaken during the Vietnam War. For more information, see A. Russo, *Comments on the Development and Implementation of a Chieu Hoi Appeal Designed to Attract Viet Cong Cadre,*" Santa Monica, Calif.: RAND Corporation, D-15661-ARPA/AGILE/IS, 1967; L. Pye *Observations on the Chieu Hoi Program*, RAND Corporation, RM-4864-1-ARPA, 1969; K. Kellen, *Conversations with Enemy Soldiers in Late 1968/Early 1969: A Study of Motivation and Morale*, Santa Monica, Calif.: RAND Corporation, RM-6131-1-ISA/ARPA, 1970; J. A. Koch, *The Chieu Hoi Program in South Vietnam, 1963–1971*, Santa Monica, Calif.: RAND Corporation, R-1172-ARPA, 1973; Chandler (1981); Page (1996).

[12] These efforts were famously termed "hearts and minds" campaigns, with the phrase originating in a speech by President John F. Kennedy.

variety of different psychological objectives, makes it relevant to today's challenges posed by terrorism.

A recurring element in the Chieu Hoi campaign was a program that used defectors (referred to as *Hoi Chanh*) to influence their peers still fighting in the field.[13] To do this, the Hoi Chanh provided recorded (written and taped) or face-to-face testimonials in an effort to exert conformational pressure on the Vietcong. Additionally, the Hoi Chanh proved to be an important source of cultural and psychological intelligence for the U.S. government.[14] The Hoi Chanh were able to identify the most effective influence efforts and characterize why they were effective, allowing U.S. officials to adjust future efforts.[15]

U.S. forces also utilized various forms of media in Vietnam. For example, the U.S. military dropped pamphlets over enemy villages and forces.[16] In the early stages of the Chieu Hoi campaign, these efforts appeared unsuccessful. Evaluations of these efforts indicate that the failure was due, in part, to a general lack of psychographic intelligence available to policymakers.[17] As a result, inappropriate language and iconography (e.g., inaccurate Vietnamese spellings and captions) as well as cultural insensitivity (e.g., ignoring nationalist sentiment) characterized the beginning of the campaign. These mistakes, in turn, allowed adversaries to easily ignore and refute the messages contained in U.S. influence operations. Some U.S. efforts did manage to successfully adapt, however, by incorporating principles of social comparison and linguistic and idiomatic appropriateness to make the influence operations more effective.

Finally, a key lesson that can be drawn from past experience in Vietnam is to expect counterpropaganda. One of the most successful

---

[13] Kellen (1970); Koch (1973); Page (1996).

[14] Koch (1973).

[15] Koch (1973).

[16] Chandler (1981); Page (1996).

[17] Kellen (1970); William Head and Lawrence Grinter, eds., *Looking Back on the Vietnam War: A 1990s Perspective on the Decisions, Combat and Legacies*, Westport, Conn.: Greenwood, 1993.

counter-messages employed by the North Vietnamese and Vietcong against U.S. forces was their depiction of the United States as an invading alien with its South Vietnamese supporters as puppets. Such counterpropaganda must be accounted for or it will effectively neutralize the friendly strategic influence attempt. As expert J. A. Koch observed in the case of Vietnam, "[U.S. forces] discounted the power of Communist agitation and armed propaganda, and they gave no priority to encouraging the Vietnamese to counter the Communist psychological warfare campaign."[18] This lesson has direct implications for the struggle against terrorism; indeed, al Qaeda has used counterpropaganda through the statements by its leadership released through Arab media networks. The lessons learned from the Chieu Hoi campaign indicate that the U.S. government should be ready to react to al Qaeda's counterpropaganda or risk losing momentum.

Eastern Europe, 1980s Polish Underground

Throughout the Cold War, American and Western European governments sought to persuade Eastern European and Soviet bloc countries to view (1) communism as oppressive and misguided, and (2) Western-style democracy and capitalism as preferable models of governance and lifestyle. The instruments for conducting these influence campaigns are well known, including Radio Free Europe, Radio Liberty, and the Voice of America.[19] Less familiar are the many clandestine influence efforts undertaken by the U.S government.[20] One of these endeavors was the U.S. government's covert support of the Polish underground media operations—e.g., the Committee for the Defense of Workers—in urban centers such as Krakow, Warsaw, and

---

[18] Koch (1973, p. 59).

[19] Short (1986); Johnson (2003); P. Taylor, *Munitions of the Mind*, Manchester, UK: Manchester University Press, 1995.

[20] See Soley (1989); R. Bathurst, *Intelligence and the Mirror: On Creating an Enemy*, Thousand Oaks, Calif.: Sage Publications, 1993; F. Saunders, *The Cultural Cold War: The CIA and the World of Arts and Letters*, New York: The New Press, 2001.

Wroclaw.[21] Insights from these covert influence campaigns further expand the options available to strategic influence planners in the struggle against terrorism.

Instead of relying exclusively on external messages produced by media outlets, such as the Voice of America, the U.S. government also provided support to local, clandestine, dissident media enterprises—termed *samizdat*. One of these enterprises was the Polish Underground, which printed dissident books, newspapers, and pamphlets off small presses hidden throughout urban areas. By supporting the samizdat, the U.S. government could advance its anticommunist message without the liability of the message being perceived as coming from an untrustworthy outsider.[22] These campaigns appear to have been successful. Indeed, many key figures in the history of the Cold War—Vaclav Havel, Lech Walesa, Mikhail Gorbachev, and Lennard Meri—credit covert support for dissident causes as a major contributor to the eventual failure of the communist movement.[23] This success was principally true in urban centers where the infrastructure and population allowed for greater numbers to be reached and converted.

The success of the Polish Underground underscores the significance of detailed cultural intelligence, especially in a covert campaign.

Alternative Methods of Influence

While media campaigns might be the most familiar persuasion techniques, the methods of influence are almost limitless. A creative example is the "Fair Play" program instituted by North American ice hockey officials in the past decade.[24] The purpose of Fair Play was to reduce the level of violence in and around hockey games. Marketing research and market segmentation analysis suggested that (1) violence

---

[21] H. G. Skilling, *Samizdat and an Independent Society in Central and Eastern Europe*, Columbus, Ohio: Ohio State University Press, 1989.

[22] See Skilling (1989) and Saunders (2001).

[23] Taylor (1995); Johnson (2003).

[24] B. Pascall and S. White, "Eliminating Violence in Hockey," Vancouver, B.C.: Ministry of Small Business, Tourism, and Culture, 2000.

on the ice was preceding violence among the spectators, (2) the players were more accessible to interventions than were spectators and parents, and (3) a long-term, consistent program of indoctrination targeted against young players could change their on-ice behaviors.[25] The resulting influence campaign included multiple, cross-supporting efforts, such as adjustments in how new players were coached, changes in actual techniques, restructuring of the reward/punishment system utilized during training, as well as posters and pamphlets in the stadiums. A study of violence in and out of the rink since the inception of Fair Play has found the campaign to be a success, as measured by the number of violence-related penalties meted out during hockey games as well as a drop in spectator violence.[26]

Although this example does not immediately appear to be relevant to the struggle against terrorism, we can draw insight from its innovation. For example, a common misconception is that influence efforts are incapable of changing hardened attitudes, as might be found with terrorists. The reasoning behind this misconception is based on the limitations of *informational social influence* (conformity): The more entrenched or "hardened" an attitude is, the more difficult it is to get an audience to think systematically about the topic through the use of information.[27] Thus, leaflets dropped over a terrorist camp that say the terrorists' cause is hopeless are not likely to be effective against the hardened militants.

The dropping-leaflets approach parallels, perhaps, the posting of bulletins around an ice hockey rink to encourage spectators not to engage in violent activities. But the hockey example illustrates the effectiveness of atypical approaches: Instead of targeting the spectators directly, Fair Play aimed at adjusting the behaviors of the players and thereby indirectly modifying the behaviors of the spectators. To apply this technique to, for example, U.S. counterterrorism policy aiming a

---

[25] Pascall and White (2000).

[26] Pascall and White (2000).

[27] Zanna "Message Receptivity: A New Look at the Old Problem of Open- vs. Closed-Mindedness," in Andrew Mitchell, ed., *Advertising Exposure, Memory, and Choice*, Hillsdale, N.J.: Erlbaum, 1990.

persuasive attempt at individuals that fund the terrorists' camp could affect, albeit indirectly, the terrorists' behavior. We would argue, therefore, that instead of dismissing influence efforts altogether, policymakers should consider atypical alternatives.

Performance Measures

As the case studies illustrate, influence programs rarely function optimally from their inception. As a result, policymakers need to measure the effectiveness of persuasive efforts and then modify their approach. Three problems make it difficult to accomplish this task. First, it is difficult to determine whether the influence operation affected the attitudes of the intended audiences. Second, it is difficult to determine whether the affected attitudes actually caused the desired behavior. Finally, attempts to measure these attitudes—and changes in attitudes—face many confounding variables.

Measuring the "emotions, motives, objective reasoning, perceptions and behaviors" of *individuals* is a well-developed art in clinical psychology. Clinicians' methods of measurement include face-to-face interviews, personality inventories, and projective tests.[28] In contrast, methods for assessing the perceptions of *populations* or *communities* are much less well developed; moreover, these perceptions appear to be more complex. It is well known that groups reflect different opinions and attitudes than do their individual members.[29] Groups also make decisions in different ways and with different outcomes than those of individuals.[30] This distinction has important implications for

---

[28] S. C. Schreiber, "Psychiatric Interview, Psychiatric History and Mental Status Exam" in Robert Hales, Stuart Yudofsky, and John Talbott, eds., *Textbook of Psychiatry*, 3rd edition, Washington, D.C: American Psychiatric Press, 1999, pp. 193–223.

[29] D. Myers and H. Lamm, "The Group Polarization Phenomenon," *Psychological Bulletin*, No. 83, 1975; Moscovici (1985).

[30] L. Festinger, "A Theory of Social Comparison Processes," *Human Relations*, No. 7, 1954; Janis (1982); D. Isenberg, "Group Polarization: A Critical Review and Meta-Analysis," *Journal of Personality and Social Psychology*, Vol. 50, No. 6, 1986; G. Herek, I. Janis, and P. Huth, "Decision-Making During International Crises: Is Quality of Process Related to

designing metrics to indicate effectiveness of an influence campaign and, therefore, deserves further exploration.

Because of the difficulty implicit in measuring attitudes, most metrics focus on behaviors. For example, policymakers might count attendance at a pro-American rally as an indicator of their success, rather than polling hard-to-reach populations. Yet even measuring changes in behavior can pose a challenge to policymakers. For example, when an enemy combatant surrenders and waves a psychological operations (PSYOPs) leaflet that guarantees "safe conduct," policymakers cannot easily determine whether the leaflet (1) caused the surrender, (2) facilitated the surrender, or (3) merely instructed the individual who is ready and willing to surrender on how to do it. Like the methods of influence, the issue of performance measures, therefore, has room for innovation.[31]

One form of metric not currently being exploited is the *marker* concept. This concept has its origins in molecular biology: The *luc* gene is used as a marker for the primary gene of interest. For example, it is difficult to determine whether certain genes have been inserted successfully into an artificial or real chromosome. To solve this problem, scientists splice the luc gene into the chromosome along with the desired gene (G). The luc gene emits a green light when it comes into contact with a chemical substrate, making it easy to identify in low light. The presence of G can, therefore, be inferred if luc is present in the chromosome.[32]

Outcome?" *Journal of Conflict Resolution*, Vol. 31, No. 2, pp. 203–226; J. Esser, "Alive and Well After Twenty-Five Years: A Review of Groupthink Research," *Organizational Behavior and Human Decision Processes*, No. 73, 1998.

[31] For more information on efforts under way to move beyond the established norms, see P. Kerchner, R. Deckro, and J. Kloeber, "Valuing Psychological Operations," *Military Operations Research*, Vol. 6, No. 2, 2001; J. Barucky, T. Connell, and B. Karabaich, "Evaluation of Cross-Cultural Models for Psychological Operations," *Report to Armstrong Lab, Human Resources Directorate*, Brooks Air Force Base, Tex., 1998; and J. Barucky, B. Karabaich, and B. Stone, *Evaluation of Cross-Cultural Models for Psychological Operations: Test of a Decision-Modeling Approach*, Rome, N.Y.: Air Force Research Laboratory, AFRL-HE-AZ-TR-2000-0158, ADA400796, Proj 1123, F41624-95-D-5030, 2001.

[32] Kenneth Luehrsen and Virginia Walbot, "Firefly Luciferase as a Reporter for Plant Gene Expression Studies," *Promega Notes*, No. 44, 1993.

This marker concept could easily be applied to persuasion attempts. For example, if policymakers wanted to determine whether a target audience is reading a magazine funded covertly by the U.S. government and, more importantly, if these same readers are being influenced by the magazine's contents, they could use markers. A small decal with the picture of the target audiences' national flag could be inserted into the magazine, urging readers to put the decal on their window or in their neighborhood as a symbol of national unity. As a marker behavior, the number of decals applied can be measured, as well as their locations and neighborhoods. Even more importantly, the decals reveal the individuals who are more likely to comply with a future urging in the periodical.[33]

The Dangers of Failure

Despite its advantages, risks are associated with the use of strategic influence. One of these risks is that influence campaigns can have unintended consequences. Persuasion is not a deterministic undertaking (such as rocketry), wherein precise calculations can predict outcomes the vast majority of the time. As a result, influence operations will occasionally lead to consequences other than, greater than, or less than anticipated. This unreliability poses a risk to policymakers, especially in the face of competing resources.

Additionally, tepid influence efforts risk ceding ground to U.S. adversaries and allowing them to control the momentum of support. For many terrorists, their survival depends on their ability to communicate effectively with supporters. As a result, many of these groups have their own active influence programs. If U.S. strategic influence is weak or lacking in the face of these campaigns, adversaries have the opportunity to sustain support or perhaps even to turn new populations against the United States.

---

[33] J. Freedman and S. Fraser, "Compliance Without Pressure: The Foot-in-the-Door Technique," *Journal of Experimental Psychology*, No. 4, 1966.

The final risk associated with strategic influence is that operations have the potential to be counterproductive. Cognitive response theory suggests that when an audience rejects a persuasion attempt, its attitudes harden even more.[34] This means that a failed influence program can be worse than useless: It can serve the adversary and make future friendly influence attempts much harder to accomplish.

Key Judgments

The practical application of influence theory is best understood through our case studies. The Chieu Hoi campaign in Vietnam highlighted the importance of investing in demographic and psychographic data at the outset of an influence operation. This planning should also account for potential counterpropaganda from adversaries, another lesson learned in Vietnam. Past experience with the Polish Underground teaches the utility of supporting indigenous movements whenever possible. Another practical lesson—drawn from post-WWII Germany—is the importance of measuring the effectiveness of influence operations and refining them overtime. Finally, the Germany case reveals that the costs and requirements of influencing widespread attitudinal change could be prohibitive.

In this chapter, we outlined a variety of different methods of persuasion. These methods include more familiar influence tools, such as cultural programs, leaflets, radio broadcasts, documentaries, and clandestine newspapers. But we also identified some uncommon approaches to persuasion, including the use of defector testimonials against hardened militants as well as the indirect application of pressure against terrorists' support communities.

What, then, can influence campaigns hope to achieve? Our research indicates that widespread attitudinal change throughout

---

[34] First outlined in Anthony Greenwald and Albert Rosita, "Acceptance and Recall of Improvised Arguments," *Journal of Personality and Social Psychology*, No. 8, 1968; A. Tesser and M. Conlee, "Some Effects of Time and Thought on Attitude Polarization," *Journal of Personality and Social Psychology*, No. 31, 1975; A. Tesser, "Self-Generated Attitude Change," in Berkowitz (1978); Lord, Ross, and Lepper (1979).

multiple communities or societies is unlikely. These conversion-type campaigns—such as General McClure's in Germany—are resource intensive and require significant control over information flows. But influence campaigns can modify the behaviors of smaller target audiences. Similarly, influence campaigns can affect a moderate shift in audiences' attitudes. We conclude this chapter with the question, "Is this enough to aid in the struggle against terrorism?" In an effort to determine the role that strategic influence can play in the struggle against terrorism, the next chapter examines the potential types of audiences in the Muslim world.

CHAPTER FOUR

Potential Audiences in the Muslim World

The Muslim world incorporates substantially diverse societies and cultures. For this reason, tension exists between designing an overall strategy for influence campaigns throughout the Muslim world and implementing such campaigns effectively in multiple discrete societies. To address this tension, we chose to focus our analysis on Muslim communities in three countries: Yemen, Germany, and Indonesia. By limiting our analysis to three countries, we can examine in detail the unique characteristics of the anti-U.S. terrorist groups and their surrounding environments.

Yemen

On October 12, 2000, two men crashed a small boat loaded with explosives into the USS *Cole*, a U.S. Navy destroyer, in Aden Harbor. The bombing killed 17 American sailors and wounded an additional 39.[1] U.S. authorities now attribute the attack to the collection of Islamic militants united under Osama bin Laden's organizational umbrella, known as al Qaeda.[2] In many ways, the significance of al

---

[1] For more information on this and other terrorist attacks, access the RAND Terrorism Chronology and the RAND-MIPT [Oklahoma City Memorial Institute for the Prevention of Terrorism] Terrorism Incident Database at http://db.mipt.org.

[2] For more information on Osama bin Laden and al Qaeda, see Bergen (2001) and Anonymous (2002).

Qaeda to Islamic militants is unclear. As discussed in Chapter One of this report, some groups act in accordance with al Qaeda, whereas others are simply affiliated, pursuing their own agendas. An examination of the USS *Cole* case provides some insight into this relationship between al Qaeda and its affiliates. But more importantly for this study, the al Qaeda cell that conducted this attack hints at the types of audiences that an influence campaign might face in the struggle against terrorism.

It now appears that the planning, preparation, and execution of the USS *Cole* attack followed along patterns similar to the 1998 U.S. embassy bombings in Kenya and Tanzania.[3] A carefully selected group was sent into Yemen to plan the attack as well as to recruit terrorists and logisticians from the local population. The final terrorist cell comprised 16 individuals, 11 of whom were Yemeni. Significantly, of these 11 Yemenis, six lived overseas, including in Saudi Arabia and the United Arab Emirates; the remaining five provided only logistical support to the cell.[4] This particular case study is interesting, therefore, because it does not appear that the impetus for the USS *Cole* attack came from local Yemeni militants. Indeed, it raises the questions, "Where and how did the six expatriate Yemenis radicalize?" and "Why did the logisticians join this group?"

It is difficult to answer these questions directly, but the wider dynamic between radical Islam, animosity toward the United States, and political violence in Yemen provides some insight. Nineteen different provinces combine to form the country of Yemen, which has a population of approximately 16 million people. Although Yemeni

---

[3] Bergen (2001); Anonymous (2002).

[4] Information on the USS *Cole* cell was taken from the following sources: "U.S.: Top al Qaeda Operative Arrested," *CNN.com*, November 22, 2002; "Alleged USS Cole Plotter Caught," *Washington Post*, November 22, 2002; "Cole Bombers Identified as Veterans of Afghan War," *Washington Post*, November 17, 2000; "Double Whammy: One ID'd in Cole Attack; 5 Indicted for Embassy Bombing," *ABCNews.com*, December 21, 2000; "USS Cole Suspect Involved in US Embassy Blast in Nairobi," *Yemen Times*, November 20, 2000; "No Connections: Bin Laden Denies Link to Cole Blast, Kuwait Plot," November 13, 2000; "Orders from Osama; Sources: Cole Suspect Believes Orders Came from bin Laden," *ABCNews.com*, January 8, 2001.

authorities claim that they administer control over 16 of these provinces, it is arguable that the central government has very little authority outside the major cities.[5] This lack of control is attributed, primarily, to the authority retained by local tribal sheikhs. Indeed, the governments in Yemen and Saudi Arabia did not even settle on a permanent border between the two countries until 2000.[6] Before that resolution, only the tribal sheikhs maintained control over the territory between the two countries, which is approximately 1,600 kilometers long and 40 kilometers wide.[7] As a result, Yemen traditionally has been a welcome haven for a variety of different militant groups, including Palestinian terrorists, weapon smugglers, and mujahideen from Afghanistan.[8]

Perhaps because of Yemen's traditional role as a haven for militants, or simply because of his Yemeni heritage, Osama bin Laden cultivated connections with a number of local sheikhs prior to the USS *Cole* attack.[9] These connections reveal one possible answer to our question, "Why did the logisticians join the al Qaeda cell?": It is likely that the leaders of the USS *Cole* cell recruited them from the local tribes. Having said that, we clarify that the links between al Qaeda and local sheikhs do not necessarily mean that the sheikhs are proponents of a radical, pan-Islamic agenda. Rather, they are fiercely independent; the more powerful sheikhs also appear to blame the West for the country's civil war and oil exploitation in the Ma'arib.[10] So while the relationship between al Qaeda and some of the powerful Yemeni tribes is an important factor in the dynamics between radical

---

[5] "Yemen Feels the Backlash," *Jane's Defence Weekly*, Vol. 38, No. 16, October 16, 2002.

[6] "Yemen Feels the Backlash" (2002).

[7] "Yemen Feels the Backlash" (2002). For information on rural Yemen, see Tim Mackintosh-Smith, *Yemen: The Unknown Arabia*, New York: Overlook Press, 2000.

[8] Sue Lackey, "Yemen: Unlikely Key to Western Security," *Jane's Intelligence Review*, October 12, 2000.

[9] Anonymous (2002, pp. 34, 126, 135–136).

[10] For information on the tribal communities in Yemen, see Mackintosh-Smith (2000) and Bowen and Early (2002). See also "Hostage to Fortune and Yemeni Guns," *The Guardian*, December 30, 1998.

Islam, political violence, and animosity toward the United States, it is not the only factor contributing to the development and success of the USS *Cole* al Qaeda cell.

Another factor appears to be the prominence of local colleges that teach radical Islam. Like the rest of the Arab peninsula, Yemenis converted to Islam in the 7th century, during Mohammad's lifetime.[11] Thus, Islamic universities and religious schools are not new to the country. But in the 1970s, as people began to migrate back and forth between Yemen and Saudi Arabia—partly a result of the expanding job market in the oil industry—Salafism (a radical subset within Sunni Islam) began to take root in Yemen.[12] With the expansion of Salafism also came the development of radical Islamic schools in Yemen. Authorities have identified at least five colleges, such as Al-Iman and Dar al-Hadith, that teach radical, pan-Islamic views. Significantly, Osama bin Laden is known to be associated with and recruit from these colleges.[13] Moreover, some of these colleges have links to mosques in Yemen's cities, such as Aden and Sana'a.[14] In these areas, bin Laden's messages and those of his supporters are spread through mosque leaders and also via cassette tapes and leaflets.[15] It is therefore possible that at least some of the individuals involved in the attack against the USS *Cole*—both the expatriates and the local recruits—were radicalized in Yemen's mosques and colleges before they left the country. During their time abroad, these Yemenis

---

[11] "Is Yemen a Conduit for Global Terrorism?" *Christian Science Monitor*, March 31, 2000; see also "Yemen: Coping With Terrorism and Violence in a Fragile State," *International Crisis Group*, January 2003.

[12] "Yemen: Coping With Terrorism and Violence in a Fragile State" (2003).

[13] See "Yemen Quakes in Cole's Shadow," *Christian Science Monitor*, September 21, 2001; "One Sheik's Mission: To Teach the Young to Despise Western Culture," *New York Times*, December 17, 2000; and Philip Smucker, "Where Holy Warriors Learn the Fundamentals," *Christian Science Monitor*, February 6, 2001.

[14] "Yemen Quakes in Cole's Shadow" (2001); "One Sheik's Mission: To Teach the Young to Despise Western Culture" (2000); Smucker (2001).

[15] The method of spreading ideas is not unique to Yemen. For more information, see Bowen and Early (2002, pp. 246–256); "From Defender of the Faith to Terrorist: Yemen's Religious Academics," *Economist*, May 30, 2002; and "Yemen Feels the Backlash" (2002).

might have then met up with like-minded individuals, associated with al Qaeda, and then returned to Yemen to plan and recruit local militants for the attack.

Two local militant groups have also played a role in the radicalization of society: the Islamic Jihad Movement (IJM) and the Aden Abyan Islamic Army (AAIA). Yemeni militants formed these and other loosely organized groups upon returning from Afghanistan. In fact, many scholars trace the escalating dynamic between support for radical Islam and political violence in Yemen back to the early 1990s and the mujahideen fighters who returned from Afghanistan.[16] The IJM and AAIA are particularly interesting because they have ties to al Qaeda. For example, Sheikh Tariq al-Fadli, a former leader of the IJM, is said to have been associated with Osama bin Laden in Afghanistan.[17] Similarly, Yemeni authorities apprehended couriers between Sheikh Abu Hamza (the London-based religious cleric recently implicated in connection with al Qaeda and the September 11, 2001, attacks) and the AAIA in 1998.[18] Subsequent to this arrest, in December 1998, AAIA members kidnapped and eventually killed three UK citizens and one Australian tourist; the leader of AAIA at the time, Zayn-al-Abidin al-Muhdar, later stated that he conducted the attacks in Osama bin Laden's name.[19] More recently, Kuwaiti authorities have accused three resident Afghan Arabs of providing money to the terrorists responsible for the October 2002 suicide boat attack against the French oil tanker *Limburg*.[20] The AAIA claimed responsibility for this last attack, but experts believe that the group

---

[16] "Yemen: Coping with Terrorism and Violence in a Fragile State" (2003); "Yemen: Unlikely Key to Western Security," *Jane's Intelligence Review*, October 12, 2000; "Rooting Out Their Radicals: Saudi Arabia, Kuwait, and Yemen Have to Admit That All Is Not As It Should Be," *The Economist*, November 21, 2002.

[17] "Yemen: Coping with Terrorism and Violence in a Fragile State" (2003); "Yemen: Unlikely Key to Western Security" (2000); "Rooting Out Their Radicals" (2002); "Hostage to Fortune and Yemeni Guns" (1998).

[18] "Yemen: Unlikely Key to Western Security" (2000).

[19] Anonymous (2002, p. 215).

[20] "Rooting Out Their Radicals" (2002).

could not have conducted the bombing successfully without outside support.[21] This series of links makes it possible that some of the five local Yemenis who provided logistical support to the USS *Cole* terrorist cell were recruited from either the IJM or the AAIA. In this instance, rather than drawing on sympathetic individuals in local colleges or support from interested sheikhs, al Qaeda members could have tapped into existing militant groups for support in carrying out its attack in Yemen.

In sum, this brief examination of the al Qaeda cell responsible for the USS *Cole* attack provides us with three different types of audiences for an influence campaign. The first audience comprises the leaders and members of the local tribal communities. These individuals may or may not be sympathetic to Osama bin Laden's radical Islamic agenda, but many apparently resent Western influence in their area of the country. Moreover, local sheikhs hold tremendous authority over their immediate communities and may interpret a relationship with Islamic militants as a way of challenging the Yemeni central government and ensuring their own independence. The second audience comprises students in local colleges and universities that teach radical Islam. This audience might not specifically articulate a desire to attack the United States, but its members are sympathetic to a radical Islamic agenda as identified by al Qaeda. As such, they present a different, but important, audience for an influence campaign. The first two audiences might or might not fight for a militant group, preferring instead to provide sanctuary, funds, or logistical support. Members of the final audience—IJM and AAIA militants—however, have already demonstrated their willingness to engage in violent activities.

---

[21] "Yemen: Coping with Terrorism and Violence in a Fragile State" (2003).

Germany

On September 11, 2001, nineteen terrorists boarded passenger planes in an effort to conduct a series of attacks against multiple targets inside the United States. Three of the four attacks succeeded: The terrorists successfully hijacked the planes and flew them into the two World Trade Center buildings and the Pentagon. The fourth plane crashed in Pennsylvania before it could reach its target. Beyond the 19 hijackers, however, various al Qaeda cells around the world provided logistical and planning support for the attack. Mohammad Atta, the operational leader of the September 11 attacks, was a member of one of these cells based in Germany, which security officials now refer to as the "Hamburg cell."[22]

What is particularly interesting about the Hamburg cell is that many of its members were from Morocco, a country that is not facing its own Islamic insurgency.[23] Also, in contrast with the Yemeni cell, the members of the Hamburg cell had been exposed to Western society and culture. This distinction raises questions about both the radicalization process of these individuals and how al Qaeda was able to persuade them to take on its anti-U.S. agenda. To answer these questions, we chose to focus on the Moroccan diaspora and its members in the Hamburg cell.

German authorities arrested Mounir el-Motassadeq in November 2001, eventually charging him with 3,000 counts of murder for his role in the September 11 attacks. German officials have identified Motassadeq, an immigrant from Marrakech, as one of six Moroccan members of the Hamburg cell, stating that "all of the members of this cell shared the same religious convictions, and Islamic lifestyle, a feeling of being out of place in unfamiliar cultural surroundings ... at the center of this stood the hatred of the world Jewry and the United

---

[22] Rohan Gunaratna, *Inside Al-Qaeda: Global Network of Terror,* New York: Columbia University Press, 2002, pp. 103–112.

[23] Like the al Qaeda cell responsible for the attack on the USS *Cole,* the Hamburg cell comprised individuals from a number of different Muslim countries. But we have decided to focus our analysis on those individuals from the Moroccan diaspora because it provides the best answers to our questions.

States."[24] Much has been made of the fact that, like many members of the Hamburg cell, el-Motassadeq was not impoverished. But little has been said about another, more relevant, aspect of the Hamburg cell: Its members had apparently radicalized *prior* to their interaction with, and recruitment into, al Qaeda. Indeed, acquaintances have testified that members of the cell frequented the city's Attawhid Islamic bookstore, debating issues such as the Palestinian *intifada* and the Gulf War.[25] Although this observation alone is not an indicator of radicalization, the bookstore is indeed known as a gathering place for individuals sympathetic to radical Islam. For example, since the September 11 attacks, German authorities have detained five individuals who met in the back room of Attawhid to discuss future martyrdom operations.[26] In addition to their links to the bookstore, members of the Hamburg cell also attended the al-Quds mosque, one of 30 mosques under the influence of radical Islamic clerics in Hamburg.[27] The al-Quds mosque frequently hosted guest speakers, such as Sheik Mohammad al-Fazazi, whom German officials suspect influenced the development of the Hamburg cell.[28] All these factors point to a progressive radicalization process among the members of the Hamburg cell; moreover, they demonstrate some hostility toward the United States prior to the members' recruitment into al Qaeda.

Notably, this radicalization process is not unique to the members of the Hamburg cell or even the Moroccan diaspora. Approximately 3.3 million Muslims live in Germany, attending one of the

---

[24] Germany's chief prosecutor, quoted in "Traces of Terror: Sept. 11 Attack Planned in '99, Germans Learn," *New York Times*, August 30, 2002.

[25] "German at Center of Sept. 11 Inquiry; Suspect Recruited Hijackers in Hamburg," *Washington Post*, June 12, 2002; "Fighting Terror: Clerics May Have Stoked Radicals' Fire," *Boston Globe*, August 4, 2002.

[26] This event occurred in July 2002. "Man Alleged to Aid 9/11 Cell Arrested in German Inquiry: Moroccan Man Assisted Hamburg Group, Officials Say," *Washington Post*, October 11, 2002.

[27] "Traces of Terror: Sept. 11 Attack Planned in '99, Germans Learn" (2002); "Clerics May Have Stoked Radicals' Fire, Qaeda Said to Use Some Radical Clerics to Help Its Cause," *Boston Globe*, August 4, 2002.

[28] "Clerics May Have Stoked Radicals' Fire" (2002).

some 2,200 prayer rooms or 77 mosques.[29] Of this 3.3 million, German authorities estimate that roughly 1 percent advocate radical Islamic views, and they have also identified 80 individuals as potential terrorists.[30] Moreover, these communities not only exist in Germany but are part of a wider North African diaspora throughout Western Europe. In his book, *Allah in the West*, Gilles Kepel discusses the history of Muslim populations in Western Europe.[31] Kepel argues that although members of this diaspora have always maintained their ties to the Muslim world, they historically have focused their activism on local issues in their country of residence, such as racism and discrimination. The 1990s, however, evidenced a shift in these communities toward a more pan-Islamic agenda.[32]

This wider dynamic throughout Western Europe sets the context for the Hamburg cell. Indeed, it now appears that the group had formed and was already articulating anti-Western views by 1997.[33] Some of the members rented an apartment together in November 1998, naming it the "House of Followers," and others moved to live nearby.[34] Around this time, the Hamburg cell became acquainted with Mohamed Heidar Zammar, an alleged al Qaeda recruiter.[35] Zammar is known to have attended the al-Quds mosque, and German authorities suspect that it was there he met and befriended

---

[29] Steffen Rink, "Under the Banner of Dialogue and Transparency: Mosques in Germany," Goethe Institute, n.d.

[30] German officials provided this information in an interview with MSNBC. The segment was titled "Germany Cracks Down on Suspects," September 11, 2002.

[31] Gilles Kepel (Susan Milner, trans.), *Allah in the West: Islamic Movements in America and Europe*, Stanford, Calif.: Stanford University Press, 1997.

[32] For a more specific account of this radicalization, see Kepel (1997, Part III, "France, Land of Islam," p. 126).

[33] "German at the Center of Sept. 11 Inquiry" (2002).

[34] "German at the Center of Sept. 11 Inquiry" (2002); "Man Alleged to Aid 9/11 Cell Arrested in German Inquiry" (2002).

[35] "Traces of Terror: The Terror Trail: German Officials Deny Knowing Whereabouts of Important Figure in Hamburg Plot," *New York Times*, June 13, 2002.

members of the Hamburg cell.[36] U.S. counterterrorism officials have stated that members of the Hamburg cell then "offered themselves" to al Qaeda, a process that apparently was facilitated through Zammar.[37] Afterward, in late 1999, Khalid Sheikh Mohammed, a key leader of al Qaeda now in U.S. custody, visited Hamburg, possibly to evaluate the members of the Hamburg cell.[38] Following his visit, in November 1999, the Hamburg cell traveled to an al Qaeda training camp near Afghanistan.[39] It is here that al Qaeda presumably augmented Mohammad Atta's group with Saudi nationals in preparation for the September 11 attacks.

It appears from this brief analysis that al Qaeda was able to take advantage of an existing dynamic between radical Islam, anti-U.S. sentiment, and some individuals' desire to engage in political violence within the Moroccan diaspora in Germany. Al Qaeda members identified a small group of individuals willing to act on their beliefs, probably through the radical mosque network in Western Europe. By bringing members of the Hamburg cell to its training camps near Afghanistan, al Qaeda could solidify the group's commitment to the September 11 attacks. Importantly, this case contrasts with our findings in the Yemeni study. For the USS *Cole* bombing, al Qaeda sent its existing members into Yemen to plan the attack and recruited locals later in the process, following the pattern of preparation for the attacks on U.S. embassies in Kenya and Tanzania.

But the Hamburg cell is also not an isolated case. Security officials have discovered similar cells throughout Western Europe. For example, in November 2001, Italian police arrested two men (also of Moroccan heritage) in Milan, accusing them of being associated with al Qaeda.[40] Both men worked at the Islamic Cultural Center in

---

[36] "Traces of Terror: The Terror Trail" (2002).

[37] "German at the Center of Sept. 11 Inquiry" (2002).

[38] "German at the Center of Sept. 11 Inquiry" (2002).

[39] "Traces of Terror: Sept. 11 Attack Planned in '99, Germans Learn" (2002); "German at the Center of Sept. 11 Inquiry" (2002).

[40] "A Nation Challenged: Men Linked to al-Qaeda Rounded Up at 2 Mosques," *New York Times*, November 30, 2001.

Milan, which also has a mosque known for its support for a radical Islamic agenda. Indeed, Italian police officials stated that they had been watching the mosque since 1995.[41] In this example, both the cultural center and the mosque parallel in circumstances with Hamburg. Security officials have also arrested suspected al Qaeda members in France. Lazahr ben Muhammad Tlilli, a Tunisian immigrant, was arrested one day after the disruption of the Milan cell. At the time of Tlilli's arrest, police discovered false documents and telephone numbers of known al Qaeda associates in his possession.[42] French officials now claim that they have identified approximately 100 people in France with ties to radical Islamic groups.[43] Although these are only examples, the discovery of these cells demonstrates that the Hamburg cell is not an isolated case but indicative of a wider dynamic in Western Europe. The relationship between radical Islam, anti-Americanism, and violence in this instance appears to be not simply the result of al Qaeda activities but a wider popular movement and, thus, a longer-term challenge for U.S. policymakers.

In sum, the Hamburg cell illustrates two additional types of audiences for a U.S. strategic influence campaign. The first audience is the leaders of mosques—specifically in the Muslim diaspora—who advocate a radical Islamic agenda. Outside the countries with a majority Muslim population, these mosques serve as the primary gathering points for like-minded Muslims. As such, not only do their leaders influence the beliefs and actions of their followers, but they also provide recruitment centers for militant groups like al Qaeda. The second audience is the wider Muslim diaspora community. Our analysis of the Hamburg cell illustrates that some members of this community feel hostility toward the United States, despite the fact that they are more familiar with it than most of the Muslim world. Of course, the U.S. government could encourage its allies to close

---

[41] "A Nation Challenged" (2001).

[42] "Threats and Responses: Arrests in Europe; Franks Links Tunisian in Jail to Terror Cells in 5 Nations," *New York Times*, October 23, 2002.

[43] "European Police Focus on North African Links; Diaspora Seen as Pool for Terror Cells," *International Herald Tribune*, September 9, 2002.

radical institutions, such as the Attawhid bookstore or al-Quds mosque, but this approach is unlikely to dissolve the relationship between anti-Americanism and radical Islam that al Qaeda was able to take advantage of in Hamburg. Our examination of the Hamburg cell also indicates that simply better articulating U.S. policy might not be enough; a refinement to the current U.S. approach might be necessary.

Indonesia

On October 12, 2002, terrorists conducted an attack against a popular nightclub in Bali. The bombing killed 187 people and was intentionally aimed at Western tourists on the island. Western authorities eventually identified the militants as members of Jemaah Islamiyah (JI), an Islamic group with a presence throughout Southeast Asia, including Indonesia, Malaysia, Singapore, the Philippines, Thailand, and Cambodia.[44] This section examines the JI and its supporters within the wider environmental context of Indonesia.

Authorities have identified two Arabs and five Indonesians responsible in the planning and implementation of the Bali attacks.[45] But the size and extent of support attributed to the JI is still unclear. Local authorities describe the group as a loose network of like-minded militant organizations, similar to a regional al Qaeda network. These authorities also believe that the JI has a leadership council comprising representatives from various militant groups—such as the Moro Islamic Liberation Front (Philippines), the Abu Sayyaf Group (Philippines), and Lashkar Jundallah (Indonesia)—with an Indonesian cleric, Abu Bakar Bashir, functioning as the group's spiri-

---

[44] Author interviews with Malaysian and Singaporean government officials, Kuala Lumpur and Singapore, August 12–15, 2003. For more information, see "Storm Clouds on the Horizon," *Far Eastern Economic Review*, February 14, 2002, and "The Danger Within," *Far Eastern Economic Review*, September 27, 2001.

[45] "Weak Link in the Anti-Terror Chain," *Far Eastern Economic Review*, October 24, 2002.

tual leader.[46] Others are suspicious of this claim and believe that the JI is a much less structured organization.[47] Yet despite this ambiguity, the JI clearly has ties to al Qaeda. Omar al-Faruq, a key al Qaeda operative, allegedly spoke about such ties to U.S. authorities upon his arrest, identifying the JI as the group behind a series of attacks against Indonesia's Catholic churches in December 2000.[48] In addition, Riduan Ismuddin, also known as Hambali and one of the JI's key operational leaders, had direct links to al Qaeda. Authorities say that Hambali (arrested in August 2003) facilitated meetings in Malaysia between al Qaeda members as they prepared for the September 11, 2001, attacks.[49] Thus, the case of the JI reveals one more possible dimension to the dynamic between radical Islam, anti-U.S. sentiment, and political violence: an organization indicative of a local insurgent group, with a local agenda, that is willing not only to provide logistical support to al Qaeda but also to cooperate with al Qaeda in its terrorist operations. Designing an influence campaign to address this dimension is a difficult but important challenge for the U.S. struggle against terrorism.

Approximately 230 million people live in Indonesia, 88 percent of whom are Muslim.[50] Yet despite the fact that well over a majority of the population is identified as Muslim, everyday life is still heavily influenced by indigenous customs. As a result, a debate exists between proponents of "cultural Islam," who essentially argue that Islam should be practiced in the household but should not be legalized, and proponents of "political Islam," who advocate the implementation of

---

[46] "What If He Isn't Guilty?" *Far Eastern Economic Review,* November 7, 2002.

[47] Author interviews with local journalists and academics, Jakarta, August 19–23, 2003.

[48] Author interviews with local journalists and academics, Jakarta, August 19–23, 2003. See also "Impact of the Bali Bombings," International Crisis Groups, Jakarta/Brussels, October 24, 2002, and "Al-Qaeda in Southeast Asia: the Case of the 'Ngruki Network' in Indonesia," International Crisis Group, Jakarta/Brussels, August 8, 2002.

[49] "Storm Clouds on the Horizon" (2002).

[50] Central Intelligence Agency, *CIA World Factbook,* July 2002, accessible at www.cia.gov/cia/publications/factbook/geos/id.html (accessed October 2004).

sharia.[51] This debate is not entirely new: It is tied to the past struggle for independence.[52] Moreover, the debate takes place in the mosques and centers of religious studies, as well as in the media (particularly on radio stations) and through pamphlets distributed from kiosks in the cities.[53] For example, one such pamphlet, named *Sabili,* has a monthly distribution of approximately 400,000.[54] *Sabili* is one of the primary advocates of anti-Americanism and political Islam. The efforts of *Sabili* and others like it are countered, on one end of the spectrum, by the Liberal Islam Network, which hosts radio shows that discuss the rationale for democracy inherent in Islam. At the other end of the spectrum, the pamphlet *Syir'ah* addresses more radical social issues; for example, the cover article in the June 2003 edition was titled "Gay Muslim." This debate sets the context for the development of and support for the JI in Southeast Asia. In the midst of this debate, a new line of argument has emerged from the radical Islamists: Islam is under siege in the region, and Muslims should fight back.

As with the other case studies, it is difficult to isolate all the factors involved in local support for the JI. Some analysts argue that a network of religious schools, termed *pesantren*, has contributed to this trend in support for Islamist groups in Indonesia.[55] The pesantren are roughly the equivalent of elementary and junior high school in the United States, but they operate outside the country's public education system. As such, they are unregulated by government authorities, and the quality and type of curricula offered varies widely. For example, some schools incorporate Islamic studies into their overall course

[51] Author interviews with local Muslim intellectuals, Jakarta, February 5, 2002.

[52] Author interviews with local pro-democracy activists and university representatives, February 5–7, 2002.

[53] Author interview with local media monitor, February 5, 2002. See also "Indonesia: Violence and Radical Muslims," International Crisis Group Indonesia Briefing Paper, October 10, 2001.

[54] Author interview with representative from an NGO that monitors religious schools and the media, August 19, 2003.

[55] For example, see "Al-Qaeda in Southeast Asia" (2002).

work, whereas others focus exclusively on religion. Because of the unregulated nature of these schools, it is difficult to gauge the extent of their influence, although experts estimate that approximately 14,000 pesantren exist, with 5 million students attending the some 4,000 pesantren that advocate political Islam.[56] Some evidence substantiates the belief that the pesantren are a factor in the increasing support for radical Islam in Indonesia. For example, a small number of these schools began to teach Salafism in the late 1990s.[57] In addition, some international nongovernmental organizations (NGOs), known for their promotion of Salafism, have taken a role in funding the pesantren as well as sponsoring their students' religious studies overseas. Termed the "radical few," these select pesantren do teach and encourage support for a radical Islamic agenda in Indonesia, if not the entire region of Southeast Asia. Yet not all of Indonesia's pesantren contribute to this radicalization process or support the JI's activities; in fact, many act as a counterbalance to the movement. Indeed, a majority of the schools teach its students cultural Islamic values. Moreover, many programs have been instituted that advocate tolerance (cultural Islam) and teach democratic processes to the students.[58] Therefore, these "radical few" pesantren are clearly not the only factor in the escalating dynamic between radical Islam, animosity toward the United States, and political violence in the region.

Local militant groups also play an important role in fostering this dynamic. Three militant organizations—in addition to the JI—operate in Indonesia. The Free Aceh Movement, or GAM, is a local insurgency based primarily in Indonesia's northwestern region, Aceh.[59] The group successfully fought for and negotiated the imple-

---

[56] Author interviews with representatives from an umbrella network of pesantren, Jakarta, February 5–7, 2002.

[57] Author interviews with local Muslim intellectuals, Jakarta, February 5, 2002.

[58] Author interviews with representatives from an umbrella network of pesantren, Jakarta, February 5–7, 2002.

[59] For a chronology of attacks by the GAM, see the RAND Terrorism Chronology and RAND-MIPT Terrorism Incident Database, available at http://db.mipt.org.

mentation of sharia in its region.[60] This success, in part, has helped fuel support for political Islam in the rest of the country. In addition, Lashkar Jihad (LJ) was involved in spiraling Christian-Muslim violence in Maluku and Ambon that began in the late 1990s. The LJ provided military training to Muslim volunteers from East and Central Java to increase the success of attacks and counterattacks against Christian communities in these areas.[61] Notably, whereas the GAM is primarily a rural-based insurgency, the LJ recruited its members from universities and urban centers.[62] Although the LJ officially disbanded in 2003, its activities contributed to the belief that Islam is under siege in the region and that Muslim activists should fight back.[63]

Finally, the Islamic Defenders Front (IDF) promotes the implementation of sharia in Indonesia. As a part of this agenda, the group's members attack local bars, stores that sell alcohol, casinos, and brothels. Unlike the GAM and LJ, the IDF's rhetoric has a substantial strain of anti-Americanism; the group also attempted to recruit volunteers to fight U.S. troops in Afghanistan.[64] So, like Yemen, Indonesia faces its own indigenous Islamic insurgency that intensifies the dynamic between radical Islam and political violence. The relationship of these two factors to anti-Americanism, however, is less clear. For supporters of the LJ and IDF, it appears that they are engaged in a struggle against outside, corrupt influences. As such, animosity toward the United States is more indirect, based on a struggle between proponents of an Islamic state versus those who support a Muslim democracy in Indonesia.

Set in this context, the JI and its supporters present a challenge to U.S. policymakers. This group has demonstrated a clear intention to attack Western targets as part of its radical Islamic agenda. The

---

[60] Author interviews with local Muslim intellectuals, Jakarta, February 5, 2002.

[61] "Indonesia: Violence and Radical Muslims" (2001).

[62] Author interviews with local Muslim intellectuals, Jakarta, February 5, 2002; "Indonesia: Violence and Radical Muslims" (2001).

[63] Author interviews with representatives from local universities and Muslim intellectuals, February 5–7, 2003.

[64] "Indonesia: Violence and Radical Muslims" (2001).

progression of JI attacks—for example, the December 2000 attacks on Catholic churches, the October 2002 Bali nightclub bombing, and the August 2003 attack on a Marriott Hotel in Jakarta—appear to illustrate this decision on the part of the JI leadership. Moreover, these attacks indicate that, far from being destroyed by counterterrorism efforts so far, the JI has been able to steadily increase its abilities to successfully target high-profile Westerners.

Yet it is also important to note that the JI has tapped into the resources of other militant groups in the region to sustain its activities. For example, the Singapore government arrested approximately 15 JI members who plotted to bomb U.S. targets in December 2001. In preparation for the attack, the group had established a cell in Singapore, accessing a network of local criminal groups.[65] Similarly, the JI apparently established contacts with local militant groups in southern Thailand; Hambali was arrested in this area in August 2003 while attempting to orchestrate attacks on U.S., British, and Israeli embassies in Bangkok.[66] Thus, the ability of the JI to tap into indigenous militant organizations, each with its own local agenda, and persuade them to cooperate with the JI indicates a more widespread and common feeling of anti-Americanism among groups in the region. This "regional al Qaeda," therefore, presents a new and emerging challenge to U.S. strategic influence and its role in the struggle against terrorism.

Our discussion of Indonesia has identified three potential audiences for a U.S. influence campaign. The first audience comprises the members of Indonesia's various militant groups, particularly the JI. Unlike in Yemen, the JI and LJ recruit from Indonesia's urban centers. Moreover, these groups have been able to take advantage of a network of media outlets that promote their agenda, including semiunderground publications and radio stations. As a result, the second audience comprises the members of nongovernmental groups that distribute the message of the Islamists, such as the "radical few"

---

[65] Author interviews with Southeast Asian security officials, August 12–20, 2003.

[66] "Hambali 'Eyed Bangkok Embassies'," *BBC News Online Edition*, August 22, 2003.

pesantren and the editors and publishers of publications like *Sabili*. The third audience comprises the wider support communities of individuals who are sympathetic to an Islamic agenda's senti- ments—such as the desire to limit the sale of alcohol or the frustra- tion aimed at outside influences—but do not support violence.

Key Judgments

Given what we have learned from these case studies, what then is the best role for strategic influence in the struggle against terrorism? Our research indicates that influence campaigns could be used, first, to break the confluence of anti-Americanism, radical Islam, and political violence within a targeted audience. We arrived at three different types of audiences: *terrorists* who attack the United States, *radical institutions* that support the terrorists, and *sympathetic communities*. In the case of Germany, the Hamburg cell falls into the terrorist cate- gory; the mosques and cultural centers are considered the radical institutions; and the Muslim activist community qualifies as sympa- thetic. Similarly, for Yemen, members of the USS *Cole* cell are the terrorists; the universities, mujahideen, and insurgencies correspond to the radical institutions that support the terrorists; and the nomadic tribes fall under the category of sympathetic communities. Finally, the JI represents Indonesia's terrorists; the pesantren, youth organizations, and NGOs form the radical institutions; and individu- als sympathetic to the LJ's activities and the implementation of sharia in the region make up the sympathetic community. Within each of these communities and categories, U.S. policymakers could design a specific campaign to interrupt the dynamic between support for radical Islam, political violence, and anti-Americanism. Doing so should—according to our analysis—reduce future support for al Qaeda and like-minded terrorists.

Figure 4.1 illustrates the three categories of audiences. It might not be possible in every instance to influence the inner circle of "ter- rorists" with an influence campaign. Yet the purpose of the figure is

Figure 4.1
Potential Sources of Animosity

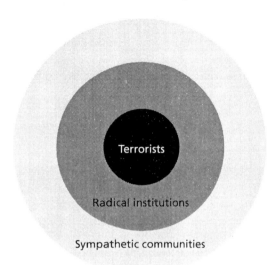

RAND *MG184-4.1*

to illustrate the interrelationship between the three audiences. Although U.S. policymakers might not be able to target the terrorists directly, influence programs that affect radical institutions or sympathetic communities may also have an indirect effect on the attitudes and beliefs of the terrorists.

The case studies emphasize that, though the *strategic* objective of a campaign might remain constant—to break the confluence of anti-Americanism, radical Islam, and political violence—the messages necessarily differ across the Muslim world. This requirement is based, in part, on the different nature of this confluence in each society. For example, in Yemen, the sheikhs' ongoing struggle to maintain their independence is a key theme. In Indonesia, this dynamic is very much related to the perception that Islam is being threatened by outside influences in the region. Finally, members of the Hamburg cell in Germany internationalized the struggle for radical Islam much more dramatically than our other case studies did.

Similarly, the methods of influence must also differ across categories of audiences and countries. Countries like Yemen, for example, do not have the widespread media culture that exists in Indonesia, so a media-based campaign is less likely to be effective. Similarly, mosques appear to be the key gathering places in Muslim diaspora communities, such as those in Germany. Yet they appear to play a diminished role in societies with a majority Muslim population, such as Indonesia. This conclusion returns us, once again, to the theory of influence: For U.S. policy to disrupt the confluence of radical Islam, violence, and anti-Americanism, both the message and the methods of a campaign must be crafted to match the intended audience.

Second, our research indicates that influence operations have the potential to exploit divergences in interests between al Qaeda and its affiliates, as well as between the terrorists, radical institutions, and wider sympathetic communities. For example, our analysis of the JI highlights the possibility that some terrorist groups could reduce support for al Qaeda's agenda if their own support is threatened by an intensive influence campaign. Even setting aside affiliated groups, al Qaeda clearly manipulated and molded the attitudes of members of the Hamburg cell and USS *Cole* cell to its own ends. Indeed, one cannot help but be impressed at the way al Qaeda was able to appeal to localized beliefs and movements in recruiting support for its attacks. A U.S. influence campaign, therefore, needs to be as sophisticated in its approach to exploiting these divergences as al Qaeda has been in overcoming them.

CHAPTER FIVE

Implications for the Struggle Against Terrorism

Our research led us to two primary observations: first, successful influence campaigns match objectives, sequencing, and methods to target audiences, and second, diverse audiences exist in the Muslim world, even among those who support al Qaeda and like-minded terrorists. We conclude that an influence campaign will need to be *flexible* to adjust to the differences between audiences' attitudes and beliefs in the Muslim world and *strategic* to account for conflicts between parallel influence operations as well as other foreign or domestic policy objectives.

In this chapter, we attempt to provide guiding principles for U.S. policymakers as they design new, and refine ongoing, influence efforts. We also explore how these principles might be applied in different operational environments, exemplified by Yemen, Germany, and Indonesia. Finally, we conclude with ways to integrate persuasion policies into the struggle against terrorism. We should point out, however, that designing influence polices that balance principles of flexibility and strategic thinking is not an easy task. Additionally, it is likely that influence campaigns will compete with other national security policies for resources. It is, therefore, not our intention to present strategic influence as a solution to the threats facing the United States today. Rather, our objective is to inform policymakers on the best use of persuasion, in light of the ongoing demands in the struggle against terrorism.

Guiding Principles

Our analysis of influence theory and past influence campaigns led us to three general principles that we believe are critical to the use of persuasion as a part of U.S. counterterrorism policy. First, design the influence campaign so that the objectives match the target audience. Our analysis revealed that overarching objectives, such as "reducing enmity toward the United States," have different policy implications for Muslim audiences. The following list translates two of our theoretical psychological objectives into specific policies:

- **Compliance:** Coerce or bribe radical institutions (e.g., schools or mosques) that facilitate terrorism or anti-American militancy to reduce that facilitation.
- **Conversion:** Support indigenous moderate and/or pluralistic Muslim movements in sympathetic communities to strengthen their momentum.

To match psychological objectives and audiences effectively, policymakers need to understand the attitudes, beliefs, opinions, and emotions of target populations. Lessons learned in Vietnam suggest that this understanding requires the use of both demographic and psychographic intelligence. Unfortunately, obtaining this type of high-quality, comprehensive intelligence is a difficult task. Yet our analysis of terrorist cells in Yemen, Germany, and Indonesia cause us to believe that this is critical to the struggle against terrorism.

Second, incorporate feedback mechanisms. Establishing these mechanisms is also a challenge. Metrics presuppose a certain degree of knowledge of the intended audiences. The U.S. government might be able to sidestep this requirement by utilizing and providing support to indigenous countermovements, as it did in the case of Poland. Yet this approach is unlikely to be possible throughout the Muslim world. In these circumstances, failure to integrate feedback mechanisms into the influence effort and adjusting policies accordingly risks losing ground to adversaries.

Finally, set realistic expectations. Our analysis of General McClure's efforts suggests that it would be very difficult—almost impossible—to duplicate Allied success in post-WWII Germany. In many ways, General McClure's tasks were much more limited than those associated with the struggle against terrorism. The target audience was less diverse than those in the Muslim world, and General McClure could control almost all the information outlets. Notably, this guideline has direct implications for ongoing efforts, such as Radio Sawa. Our analysis indicates that this campaign and others like it are less likely to have a significant impact on future terrorism against the United States.

Translating the Principles into Policy

Despite the limitations and risks, we conclude that influence campaigns could be used to disrupt the convergence of political violence, radical Islam, and animosity toward the United States. Strategic influence could also be used to exploit the divergence of interests between terrorists, radical institutions, and sympathetic communities in the Muslim world. Moreover, our analysis of Yemen, Germany, and Indonesia suggests that these policies will likely reduce the threat of terrorism. This section takes the next step: Treating the three Muslim communities as representatives of the types of audiences that a campaign might encounter, we suggest some general approaches to applying our principles in an operational setting.

Multiple al Qaeda–Affiliated Groups in Societies Hostile to Outsiders

Yemen represents one type of operational environment that policymakers could face when designing an influence campaign as part of the struggle against terrorism. In Yemen, the local terrorist groups sometimes cooperate with each other as well as with other international terrorists. The al Qaeda cell responsible for the USS *Cole* attack represents some of the terrorists. But there are other groups in Yemen linked with al Qaeda, including the IJM and AAIA. In addition, radical institutions that sympathize with al Qaeda's pan-Islamic agenda—

including five known colleges and loose collections of mujahideen—provide the terrorist organizations with recruits. Finally, nomadic tribes control a significant portion of Yemen and allow terrorists to recruit, train, and operate in relative safety. Many of the tribal sheikhs are not sympathetic to al Qaeda's pan-Islamic agenda, but they resent outside influence and blame the West for the country's civil war and oil exploitation in the Ma'arib.

With hardened attitudes, terrorists are less vulnerable to direct persuasion efforts. The USS *Cole* cell presents an even greater challenge because it formed and then dissolved after one specific attack. It therefore would be difficult and probably futile to attempt direct methods of changing the attitudes, beliefs, interests, and/or opinions of individuals in other similar cells.

Having said that, our research demonstrated that terrorists are embedded in a matrix of other institutions. It is likely that these institutions will be more susceptible to persuasive efforts. For example, like-minded militant groups in Yemen, such as the AAIA and IJM, provided logistical support to the al Qaeda cell. A persuasion campaign directed at these groups could, for example, reduce their willingness to cooperate with al Qaeda, thereby indirectly affecting future attacks against the United States.

Another indirect approach could target the relationship between local militants, radical institutions, and sympathizers. For example, the U.S. government could take advantage of the unreliable relationship between the local tribes and terrorists in Yemen. Some tribal sheikhs appear to be supporting the terrorists out of a general hostility to Western influence in their region as well as for material benefit. An influence effort aimed at reducing tribal support for anti-U.S. terrorism therefore would not have to reeducate tribe members or alter their group dynamics. Instead, an effort to persuade these sheikhs—through inducements—to reduce support for terrorists and to encourage their followers to do likewise could curtail terrorist attacks or at least reduce the terrorists' overall capabilities.

Isolated al Qaeda Cells in Western Societies

In Germany, the Hamburg cell was similar to the USS *Cole* cell in that it did not have to sustain activities beyond its attack. Yet, unlike the USS *Cole* cell, the Hamburg cell initially formed outside al Qaeda's influence; al Qaeda focused and enabled the cell's political violence but did not initiate it. Most of the Hamburg cell's radicalization took place without, for example, the sequestration of a paramilitary training camp. This suggests that members of the Hamburg cell were exposed to a variety of Western and non-Western media, many of which were neither exponents of radical Islam nor virulently anti-American.

In media-rich societies, a wide range of options is available to the policymaker, including television, radio, newspapers, religious tracts, and discussion groups. In an attempt to dissuade potential recruits, for example, support could be provided to Islamic study groups that do not espouse violence. Importantly, the objective of these campaigns should not be to persuade individuals to become advocates of U.S. foreign policy but rather to deflect the behaviors of radicals like the members of the Hamburg cell into other, less-violent forms of anti-Americanism.

Additionally, we identified the wider Islamist activist community in Germany as part of the "sympathetic community" audience. Animosity toward the United States is part of the wider political culture in Germany, and therefore "sympathetic communities" should be understood in that environmental context. Yet it is clear that the members of the Hamburg cell moved freely and lived within this wider community, sustaining a potent belief system that included radical Islam, political violence, and hatred of the United States. A long-term campaign to shape the media presence of radical Islam could play an important role in dissuading support for terrorism in this type of wider sympathetic community.

Multiple Terrorist Groups with an Indigenous Countermovement

Indonesia—and the Bali and Marriott attacks therein—provides a different, yet important, example of the type of audience that a persuasive effort might confront in the struggle against terrorism. The JI

functions much like a regional al Qaeda, providing an umbrella organization to pull in other like-minded groups in Indonesia and
throughout Southeast Asia. Indeed, many terrorist groups under the
JI umbrella demonstrate all three characteristics that pose a threat to
U.S. interests: espousing radical Islam, enmity toward the United
States, and a propensity for political violence. Yet the diversity of
groups also creates a number of opportunities for strategic influence.

For example, many of the leaders of the various terrorist groups
under the JI umbrella have their own agendas. Instead of focusing
specifically on reducing animosity toward the United States, U.S.
efforts could attempt to weaken the propaganda operations of the terrorist groups. Once again, the purpose of these campaigns should be
to present individuals with legitimate alternatives to the activities and
philosophies advocated by groups like the JI.

In addition, Indonesia has a number of institutions that promote enmity toward the United States and advocate violence,
including some 4,000 pesantren (religious schools). Some local
groups have begun countering this influence by introducing classes
on pluralism into many of the religious schools. Support for these
efforts has the potential to reduce the pool of new recruits for al
Qaeda–affiliated organizations like the JI as well as for al Qaeda itself.
We are not suggesting that, at the end of the campaign, audiences
will be advocates of U.S. foreign policy. Instead, the goals of such a
campaign should be far more achievable, such as widening the set of
perceived options for self-expression from violence alone to violence
plus other options.

Potential Risks and Mitigating Strategies

Clearly, there are risks associated with even the simple persuasive
campaigns discussed above. For example, programs designed to
strengthen the momentum of an indigenous, nonviolent movement
could reduce its credibility if discovered. Or even successful counterpropaganda efforts that weaken a terrorist group's anti-Americanism
could accidentally shift animosity onto an important ally. Accurate

performance measures can provide decisionmakers with early warnings for adverse consequences. But it is important to acknowledge that strategic influence efforts—from diplomacy to psychological operations—have some uncertainty.

Similarly, we discussed in Chapter One how military objectives and persuasion efforts can often conflict. Recall the example of Iraq, in which the U.S. military secured individuals by placing bags over their heads and forcing them to kneel in front of their families. This approach might be effective from a short-term information-gathering perspective, but it can adversely affect persuasion efforts in the area. This example illustrates the importance of intelligence, planning, and performance measures. It also suggests the importance of coordination between U.S. government entities so that decisionmakers can evaluate and attempt to mitigate all the potential risks. This coordination should include the State Department and intelligence organizations, as well as the Civil Affairs component of the military and Special Operations Forces.

Finally, we emphasize that influence policies, such as the ones described above, do not operate in a vacuum. After the September 11, 2001, attacks, the U.S. government instituted a number of new foreign and domestic policies—for example, the registering of temporary residents from some Muslim countries in the United States—that have received significant attention in the Muslim world. Influence campaigns have to operate in the midst of this environment. We chose to use the term strategic influence to convey this reality. Our analysis indicates that influence campaigns can deflect potential new recruits and support for terrorist attacks against the United States, but only to the extent that other U.S. policies do not overwhelm the positive momentum created by these campaigns.

CHAPTER SIX

New Challenges Ahead

Three years after the September 11, 2001, attacks, the U.S. government is still struggling with exactly how to wage a war on terrorism. Billions of dollars have been committed to the issue, including military operations in Afghanistan and homeland security grants for state and local responders. Yet it is arguable that the threat of terrorism is as real and pervasive today as it was on September 10, 2001. It is a sobering thought. Despite the fact that the United States and its allies have removed a key state sponsor of terrorism from power (the Taliban), arrested numerous members of al Qaeda and its affiliated groups, and heightened protection activities around the world, radical Islamic terrorists continue their attacks. So what can the U.S. government do to reduce the threat of terrorism?

It is doubtful that this report—or any other study—can provide a complete answer to this question. Indeed, RAND analysts have been studying terrorism and counterterrorism tactics for more than 30 years. These studies include analyses of specific groups, such as Gordan McCormick's work on the Shining Path.[1] They also include strategic analyses for understanding emerging threats, such as the study by Bonnie Cordes et al. titled *A Conceptual Framework for*

---

[1] Gordan McCormick, *The Shining Path and the Future of Peru*, Santa Monica, Calif.: RAND Corporation, R-3781-DOS/OSD, 1990; Gordan McCormick, *From the Sierra to the Cities: The Urban Campaign of the Shining Path*, Santa Monica, Calif.: RAND Corporation, R-4150-USDP, 1992.

Analyzing Terrorist Groups in 1985[2] or Ian Lesser et al.'s *Countering the New Terrorism* in 1999[3]. Yet no one has discovered a "silver bullet" to remove the threat of terrorism. Moreover, it is difficult to imagine that strategic influence could be the solution. As with terrorism, RAND analysts have long evaluated the potential strengths and weaknesses of U.S. military PSYOPs. The bibliography to this report alone includes seven RAND studies on the topic of persuasion and PSYOPs. If there is one overarching theme to these studies, it is that influence is a complex and difficult process—hardly a silver bullet.

As we embarked on this study, we were surprised by how little research was being done on the role of persuasion in the struggle against terrorism. Even in an institution such as RAND, with a long history of research on both issues, the only recent study that merges the two disciplines is Paul Davis and Brian Jenkins' *Deterrence and Influence in Counterterrorism* (2002), which focuses on deterrence and not the full range of strategic influence. So we determined to combine our separate knowledge of terrorism and persuasion in an effort to explore the parameters of influence specifically with regard to U.S. counterterrorism policy.

But this study only goes so far. Significant gaps still exist in the study of terrorism and persuasion that make it difficult to combine the two disciplines. For example, we mentioned previously that very little is known about measuring, and therefore truly understanding, *group* versus *individual* perceptions. It is arguable that terrorist groups, rather than individual actors, pose the greatest threat to the United States. So this lack of knowledge hinders U.S. policymakers' ability to successfully implement influence campaigns against terrorist groups. Similarly, from a counterterrorism viewpoint, we know very

---

[2] Bonnie Cordes, Brian Michael Jenkins, Konrad Kellen, Gail V. Bass-Golod, Daniel A. Relles, William F. Sater, Mario L. Juncosa, William Fowler, and Geraldine Petty, *A Conceptual Framework for Analyzing Terrorist Groups*, Santa Monica, Calif.: RAND Corporation, R-3151, 1985.

[3] Ian O. Lesser, Bruce Hoffman, John Arquilla, David F. Ronfeldt, and Michele Zanini, *Countering the New Terrorism*, Santa Monica, Calif.: RAND Corporation, MR-989-AF, 1999.

little about the internal dynamics of terrorist groups—for example, how they make decisions and, more importantly, what causes shifts in their ideology and target choices. Again, this lack of knowledge limits counterterrorists' ability to deflect attacks away from U.S. interests. Finally, much more could be done to explore the wave of anti-Americanism evident in the world, examine how this affects the U.S. war on terrorism, and determine what could be done to mitigate the problem. Despite this critique, policymakers and analysts are making progress. As such, this report should be viewed as one in a long series of studies—in the past and future—that contribute to an understanding of the role of persuasion in counterterrorism.

The Military Perspective on Strategic Influence

In military terms, strategic influence programs are psychological operations (PSYOPs) conducted at the strategic and political levels. PSYOPs are defined as

> planned operations to convey selected information and indicators to foreign audiences to influence their emotions, motives, objective reasoning, and ultimately the behavior of foreign governments, organizations, groups, and individuals. The purpose of psychological operations is to induce or reinforce foreign attitudes and behavior favorable to the originator's objectives.[1]

There are several points to highlight in this definition. First, there is flexibility. The target of PSYOPs is defined as "foreign audiences," which could mean a small band of insurgents, a large group of journalists, a massive population under the age of 40, or anything else. The key issue is that the "foreign audience" in question must have been identified previous to the PSYOP effort as possessing some ability or inclination of importance to the friendly military effort. For example, to keep children at home and away from school, a PSYOP planner might identify child-rearing mothers as the "foreign audience" to be targeted, knowing that these mothers can restrain the children from leaving for school. "Foreign audiences" can also include enemy combatants, as well as their active and passive supporters.

---

[1] U.S. Joint Chiefs of Staff (1996).

Classic uses of PSYOPs focus intently on this type of "foreign audience" and include the leaflet dropped on—or loudspeaker blared to—enemy troops urging them to surrender.

Second, there is what we might call end-to-end psychological targeting. The phrase "emotions, motives, objective reasoning, and ultimately behavior" is an attempt to encompass the full range of mental and physical processes, which might be targeted by PSYOPs. The authors prefer the terms more commonly used in the psychological literature to describe this range of processes: perceptions, cognitions, and behaviors. Note that there is an implied directionality to these terms (i.e., perceptions to cognitions to behaviors) and that they can generally be seen to encompass the full range of mental processes involved in decisionmaking. That is, *perceptions* are mental representations of the world; *cognitions* include attitudes, opinions, emotions, motivation, and reasoning; while behaviors are just that— behaviors. By defining PSYOPs as able to target any of these steps, myriad tools become available to create the desired effect. Importantly, it is critical to recognize that *different* tools are appropriate at different stages.

Third, there are many possible success conditions for PSYOPs. Desirable behaviors loom large as among the most important of success metrics—i.e., Did the target do what we wanted?—but perceptions and cognitions are critical as well. To illustrate the point, a desired behavior during offensive missions ("Do not fire on U.S. troops advancing through the city...") might be gained by means of significant coercion ("...or we will kill you.") but leave cognitions untouched ("I hate those Americans...") or even worsened ("...more than ever...") and engender future difficulties ("...and will attack them when they begin their occupation."). Thus it is important to note that, by definition, PSYOPs can be applied to many perceptions, cognitions, and behaviors and that the impact can be measured and judged successful at each level, depending on the PSYOP planner's agenda.

Fourth, there is the virtually infinite variety of means that may be harnessed for PSYOP ends. The definition states that PSYOPs aim to "convey selected information and indicators" to the target but is not in any way specific as to what that information or those indicators need be, nor how it should be conveyed. This ambiguity is both liberating and dangerous: The PSYOP planner can employ virtually any means (radio, rumor, pamphlet, graffiti, movie, email, etc.) to convey any kind of information or indicator (news, propaganda, warnings, slander, instructions, timetables, etc.).

It should be obvious that many of the aspects of PSYOPs, which make them so valuable in conflict, are applicable to strategic influence campaigns in peace, crisis, and war.

Relationship Between PSYOPs and Other Military Activities

Some military functions are closely related to PSYOPs. For example, *civil affairs* are defined as

> the activities of a commander that establish, maintain, influence, or exploit relations between military forces and civil authorities, both governmental and nongovernmental, and the civilian populace in a friendly, neutral, or hostile area of operations in order to facilitate military operations and consolidate operational objectives. Civil affairs may include performance by military forces of activities and functions normally the responsibility of local government. These activities may occur prior to, during, or subsequent to other military actions. They may also occur, if directed, in the absence of other military operations.[2]

Note that by this definition, the term "civil affairs" includes the objective of cultivating and shaping the relations between the full range of civilians and friendly military forces. Clearly, this objective is very much like the PSYOP objective of inducing/shaping attitudes and behaviors in civilian populations that are advantageous to friendly forces. The two most important areas of difference between civil affairs and PSYOPs are the following:

---

[2] U.S. Joint Chiefs of Staff, *Department of Defense Dictionary of Military and Associated Terms*, Joint Publication 1-02, 2004.

- PSYOPs include enemy military personnel in their potential target audiences, whereas civil affairs do not.
- Civil affairs activities include employing friendly forces in civilian roles, whereas PSYOPs are concerned exclusively with the transmission of information to achieve persuasive ends. (As an aside, the authors note that employing friendly forces in civilian roles will frequently have a psychological impact as great or greater than any PSYOP could effect.)

Another military activity related to PSYOPs is *public affairs*. Public affairs activities are

> those public information, command information, and community relations activities directed toward both the external and internal publics with interest in the Department of Defense.[3]

Public affairs activities are roughly equivalent to news reporting in their dissemination of factual information related to military forces and operations. The critical distinction between public affairs and PSYOPs is that the latter are not directed at domestic (U.S.) audiences. When public affairs are directed at external (non-U.S.) audiences, they are virtually indistinguishable from PSYOPs. Some have argued for another distinction: Public affairs are not meant to be persuasive, whereas PSYOPs are. However, the authors believe that public affairs are an example of *informational social influence*,[4] just as any other media reporting is. Definitions of public affairs that claim its role is not meant to propagandize are idealistic and not based on content analyses of public affairs products.[5] That said, influencing audiences through high-quality news reporting is a good thing, and not at all pernicious. When planned and conducted effectively, public affairs

---

[3] U.S. Joint Chiefs of Staff (2004).

[4] As defined previously, individuals cue their decisionmaking off facts or information (e.g., news reports) and adjust their behavior accordingly.

[5] See content analyses of military reporting by media-watch organization Fairness and Accuracy In Reporting.

can be exceedingly valuable: playing a vital role in risk communication between government officials and citizenry, for example. Although a detailed analysis of public affairs is beyond the scope of this report, it should suffice to say that virtually all the principles that govern PSYOPs apply to public affairs. For military and civilian officials charged with protecting the United States (e.g., those of the Department of Homeland Security or the U.S. Northern Command), this point is important to note.

A third military activity closely related to PSYOPs is *deception*, defined as

> those measures designed to mislead *relevant decision-makers*[6] by manipulation, distortion, or falsification of evidence to induce him/her to react in a manner prejudicial to his/her interests.[7]

PSYOPs and deception differ in two main respects: falsity and scale. Deception always seeks inaccurate perception in the mind of the target, whereas PSYOPs can seek accurate perceptions, inaccurate perceptions, or any kind of admixture of the two. If the objective of a PSYOP is to engender an inaccurate belief in the minds of a large population, then it is virtually identical to deception; however, PSYOPs can be just as effective—perhaps more so—when conveying information in such a way as to engender accurate perceptions in the target's mind. The second, and more consistent, distinction between the two is a difference in targeting: Deception as a military activity is most often aimed at the mind of one or a few enemy decisionmakers (or one or a few influential individuals whose actions will directly affect military outcomes), whereas PSYOPs are aimed at much larger populations (orders of magnitude larger, usually). Thus, both deception and PSYOPs can affect consequences at all levels of war: decep-

---

[6] Emphasis added. For an explanation of why "enemy" should be replaced with "relevant decision-makers," see S. Gerwehr and R. Glenn, *The Art of Darkness*, Santa Monica, Calif.: RAND Corporation, MR-1132-A, 2000, and S. Gerwehr and R. Glenn *Unweaving the Web*, Santa Monica, Calif.: RAND Corporation, MR-1495-A, 2003.

[7] U.S. Joint Chiefs of Staff (2004).

tion does so through influencing a few, whereas PSYOPs influence many.

The last military function we relate to PSYOPs is the umbrella term *information operations* (IO), which are

> actions taken to affect adversary information and information systems while defending one's own information and information systems.[8]

Clearly, by this definition, IO include and overlap public affairs, PSYOPs, deception, and many components of civil affairs. PSYOPs are subsumed entirely under the aegis of IO; therefore, responsibility for the planning, conduct, analysis, and management of PSYOPs come under the authority of IO personnel.

In reflecting on the connection between PSYOPs and these other related military activities, two critical issues emerge. First, given that these other activities deliberately interact with the noncombatant population of an operations area and include changing and managing noncombatant attitudes and behaviors as part of their raison d'etre, it is vital that the planning and execution of PSYOP be tightly integrated with the planning and execution of these other activities. This means more than just de-conflicting the activities but truly coordinating them for maximum benefit to all. Although this point might seem obvious on its face, it has often been overlooked or under-appreciated: Many historical examples exist that illustrate both the benefits of integration and the significant costs that accrue when these activities are at cross-purposes with each other. For example, in the 1982 invasion of Lebanon, the Israeli Defense Forces (IDF) used PSYOPs to encourage Lebanese residents of Sidon and Tyre to leave the cities and move to "safe havens" on the beach. The goal of this PSYOP was an important one—separating noncombatants from Palestine Liberation Organization fighters—and by use of radio and leaflet drops, the IDF did manage to get many noncombatants to leave for the beaches. However, IDF civil affairs had failed to provide

---

[8] U.S. Joint Chiefs of Staff (2004).

sufficient accommodations for the refugees, and shortly after arriving and overwhelming the modest logistical capabilities that the IDF civil affairs had put in place, the noncombatants streamed back into their cities with (1) increased enmity for the Israelis, and (2) decreased confidence in the credibility of IDF PSYOPs.[9]

Second, there are many activities outside the IO realm that still have a significant impact on the conduct and impact of PSYOPs. The most obvious example is that of combat: If coalition troops are firing on anything that moves, without rules of engagement, the noncombatant casualties certain to arise will likely interfere with PSYOPs intended to convince the local populace that friendly forces mean them no harm. Lt. Gen. Ricardo Sanchez captures this point:

> ...we had to go out there and do these big sweeps. Unquestionably, I think, we created in this culture some Iraqis that had then to act because of their value systems against us in terms of revenge, possibly because there were casualties on their side and also because of the impact on their dignity and respect.[10]

This mind-set is well understood (although, as illustrated by the above example, still difficult to contend with) by combatant commanders who deploy forces into hot spots overseas. Less appreciated, though exceedingly important, is the psychological impact of combat service and combat service support functions outside IO. For example, consider supply: When trucks are dispatched to supply front-line troops in urban areas with food, fuel, ammunition, and the like, their choice of route is usually determined by expediency and safety. But another factor exists: the psychological impact of that supply movement. Trucks driving up and down residential streets in the middle of the night can alienate and anger residents. Or a worse scenario: Trucks racing up and down streets to minimize chances of being fixed for an ambush could strike a child and create a very negative

---

[9] R. D. McLaurin, *The Battle of Sidon*, Aberdeen Proving Ground, Md.: U.S. Army Human Engineering Laboratories, 1989.

[10] "To Mollify Iraqis, US Plans to Ease Scope of Its Raids" (2003).

public relations debacle. But there is as much positive as negative potential here for the trucks and the troops manning them to interact with the populace in a large-scale and direct manner that can complement the work of civil affairs, public affairs, PSYOPs, etc. A supply truck could sideswipe and damage a civilian vehicle and move on, as described in the example above; alternatively, it could stop and render assistance to the motorist stranded on the road. Though clearly not without risk, there are certainly a large number of opportunities for managing noncombatant attitudes and actions inherent in military activities well beyond those designated as IO. The overall joint force commander, for example, should plan to coordinate *all* the tools available for psychological effect. The key point is that this includes virtually every instrument available, not just the ones included under the IO umbrella.

Strategic Influence in Action: Advertising and Marketing

It has long been recognized that strategic influence bears a strong resemblance to some kinds of advertising[1] and social marketing[2]. We find this comparison useful and believe that much of the "doctrine" of advertising and marketing is highly prescriptive for strategic influence purposes.

Advertising

Introducing new ideas and new behaviors into a target population is not an easy task. Yet it is a recurring challenge for strategic influence personnel, who may be trying, for example, to sever a longstanding tie between an insurgent group and its base of popular support, inculcate new political thinking in a liberated population, or even reduce ethnic strife in an area wracked by sectarian violence. The field of advertising has a wealth of prescriptive knowledge on the topic of breaking into new markets of thought and action; as such, it should be mined by those responsible for the planning, execution, management, and measurement of strategic influence.

For example, one of the methods that savvy advertisers rely on when cracking open new markets is termed the *foot-in-the-door* tech-

---

[1] Defined as "Description or presentation of a product, idea, or organization, in order to induce individuals to buy, support, or approve of it" (www.investorwords.com).

[2] Defined as "Drawing on the process by which products and services are introduced to the marketplace and applying these lessons to programs to effect attitudinal and behavioral change in a target population" (www.investorwords.com).

nique of persuasion. This phenomenon was first described by social psychologists and then put into practice by advertisers (a very common pattern in the history of advertising). Essentially, foot-in-the-door refers to the increased likelihood of a subject complying with a second request if he or she complies with the smaller first request. In fact, we suggest this approach in our discussion of the luc gene and markers, in Chapter Three. There, we propose the idea that policymakers could use a national flag icon as a marker for individuals who read a particular magazine, asking readers to place the flag in their windows. But we further indicate that those markers also identify individuals most likely to act on future suggestions printed in the magazine. The pioneering experimental work on this phenomenon was done by Freedman and Fraser.[3] Subsequently, other researchers have shown it to be effective across activities such as fund-raising[4] and critically have found the effect to obtain even when the follow-up request is unrelated to the initial request[5].

This latter point is a perfect example of how strategic influence planners can draw from market research and social psychological studies: If a strategic influence goal is to have a target audience read a pamphlet (e.g., instructions on surrender and processing, or laws promulgated by the U.S. occupation force), a useful tactic would be to first get target audiences to read a simple, useful leaflet (e.g., a schedule of forthcoming air strikes) or even just to pick up air-dropped food containers. The likelihood of reading the subsequent pamphlet increases in both cases. Notably, the goal of this approach is not to adjust the subjects' attitudes vis-à-vis the United States, but rather to affect their actions.

---

[3] Freedman and Fraser (1966).

[4] J. Schwarzwald, A. Bizman, and M. Raz, "The Foot-in-the-Door Paradigm: Effects of Second Request Size on Donation Probability and Donor Generosity," *Personality and Social Psychology Bulletin*, No. 9, 1983.

[5] M. Snyder and M. R. Cunningham, "To Comply or Not to Comply: Testing the Self-Perception Explanation of the Foot in the Door Phenomenon," *Journal of Personality and Social Psychology*, No. 31, 1975.

Clearly, there are many advertising principles beyond foot-in-the-door that apply to strategic influence. A detailed discussion of advertising is beyond the scope of this report. However, the key point is simply that strategic influence is (1) related in both theory and practice to advertising, and (2) likely to benefit greatly from an infusion of advertising knowledge and guidance—not personnel, but precepts.

Social Marketing

For three decades, researchers and practitioners alike have sought to apply the proven techniques of marketing toward ends apart from business. As Andreasen notes:

> they recognized that the basic goal of marketing is to influence behavior, whether that behavior is buying a Big Mac, flying United Airlines, practicing safe sex, or getting one's child immunized (Andreasen, 1993).[6] In each case, marketers mount programs to bring about these behaviors. Some programs, like that of United Airlines or the National High Blood Pressure Education Program, are very long term. Others, like many new cereal introductions and some health care interventions, are shorter lived.[7]

Two of the most important attributes of social marketing programs are market research[8] conducted before the program begins and market segmentation[9] that are used to get specific messages to specific audiences.[10] Social marketing eschews the "broadcasting" approach in

---

[6] Alan R. Andreasen, "A Social Marketing Research Agenda for Consumer Behavior Researchers," in Leigh McAlister and Michael L. Rothschild, eds., *Advances in Consumer Research*, Provo, Utah: Association for Consumer Research, 1993, pp. 1–5.

[7] Fishbein, Goldberg, and Middlestadt (1997).

[8] Defined as "The collection and analysis of information about consumers, market niches, and the effectiveness of marketing programs" (www.investorwords.com).

[9] Defined as "A marketing technique that targets a group of customers with specific characteristics" (www.investorwords.com).

[10] M. Weiss, *The Clustering of America*, New York: Harper & Row, 1988; M. Riche, "Psychographics for the 1990s," *American Demographics*, July 1989.

favor of a more finely resolved view of the audience, as well as a more nuanced view of how the persuasive message ought to be crafted and delivered. When used effectively, social marketing can be a powerful tool for influencing the attitudes and behaviors of target audiences, both directly and indirectly.

Once again, we draw on this experience in previous chapters as well. For example, we suggest that policymakers match the appropriate message with target audiences. This approach, we note, requires detailed psychographic and demographic intelligence. In essence, this requirement is the first step in achieving market segmentation. Yet much more could be gleaned from the discipline of social marketing. Indeed, social marketing is not only an endeavor similar to strategic influence, but it should also be a source of both theoretical and practical guidance to all those who plan, execute, manage, and measure strategic influence. This is particularly true for longer-term interventions, focused on changing cognitions (attitudes, values, emotions) in the target audience.

Bibliography

Works Cited

"A Nation Challenged: Men Linked to al-Qaeda Rounded Up at 2 Mosques," *New York Times*, November 30, 2001.

"Al-Qaeda in Southeast Asia: The Case of the 'Ngruki Network' in Indonesia," International Crisis Group Report, Jakarta/Brussels, August 8, 2002.

"Alleged USS Cole Plotter Caught," *Washington Post*, November 22, 2002.

Altman, I., and D. Taylor, "Communication in Interpersonal Relationships: Social Penetration Theory," in Roloff and Miller (1987, pp. 257–277).

Andreasen, Alan R., "A Social Marketing Research Agenda for Consumer Behavior Researchers," in McAlister and Rothschild (1993, pp. 1–5).

_____, *Marketing Social Change: Changing Behavior to Promote Health, Social Development, and the Environment,* San Francisco: Jossey-Bass, 1995.

Anonymous, *Through Our Enemies Eyes*, Washington, D.C.: Brassey's, 2002.

Asch, S. E., "Effects of Group Pressure upon the Modification and Distortion of Judgment," in Guetzkow (1951).

Asch, S. E., "Studies of Independence and Conformity: A Minority of One Against a Unanimous Majority," *Psychological Monographs*, Vol. 70, No. 416, 1956.

Bandura, A., *Principles of Behavior Modification*, New York: Holt, Rinehart and Winston, 1969.

Barucky, J., T. Connell, and B. Karabaich, "Evaluation of Cross-Cultural Models for Psychological Operations," *Report to Armstrong Lab, Human Resources Directorate*, Brooks Air Force Base, Tex., 1998.

Barucky, J., B. Karabaich, and B. Stone, *Evaluation of Cross-Cultural Models for Psychological Operations: Test of a Decision Modeling Approach*, Rome, N.Y.: Air Force Research Laboratory, AFRL-HE-AZ-TR-2000-0158, ADA400796, Proj 1123, F41624-95-D-5030, 2001.

Bathurst, R., *Intelligence and the Mirror: On Creating an Enemy*, Thousand Oaks, Calif.: Sage Publications, 1993.

Bergen, Peter, *Holy War, Inc.*, New York: Columbia University Press, 2001.

Berger, C. R., and S. H. Chafee, eds., *The Handbook of Communication Science*, Newbury Park, Calif.: Sage Publications, 1987.

Berkowitz, L., ed., *Advances in Experimental Social Psychology*, New York: McGraw-Hill, 1964.

Bowen, Donna Lee, and Evelyn A. Early, eds., *Everyday Life in the Muslim Middle East*, 2nd edition, Bloomington, Ind.: Indiana University Press, 2002.

Borgatta, E., and W. Lambert, eds., *Handbook in Personality Theory and Research*, Chicago: Rand McNally, 1968.

"Bush Hails Capture of Top al-Qaeda Operative," *CNN.com*, May 1, 2003.

Bryson, Lyman, ed., *The Communication of Ideas*, New York: Harper & Row, 1948.

Campbell, J., A. Tesser, and P. Fairey, "Conformity and Attention to the Stimulus: Temporal and Contextual Dynamics," *Journal of Personality and Social Psychology*, No. 51, 1986, pp. 315–324.

Cartwright, D., and A. Zander, eds., *Group Dynamics: Research and Theory*, Evanston: Peterson and Co., 1953.

Central Intelligence Agency, *CIA World Factbook*, July 2002.

Chaiken, S., "The Heuristic Model of Persuasion," in Zanna, Olson, and Herman (1987, Vol. 5, pp. 3–39).

Chaiken, S., and A. Eagly, "Communication Modality as a Determinant of Message Persuasiveness and Message Comprehensibility," *Journal of Personality and Social Psychology*, Vol. 34, 1976, pp. 605–614.

Chaiken, S., A. Liberman, and A. H. Eagly, "Heuristic and Systematic Information Processing Within and Beyond the Persuasion Context," in Uleman and Bargh (1989, pp. 212–252).

Chandler, R., *War of Ideas: The U.S. Propaganda Campaign in Vietnam*, Boulder, Colo.: Westview, 1981.

"Clerics May Have Stoked Radicals' Fire; Qaeda Said to Use Some Radical Clerics to Help Its Cause," *Boston Globe*, August 4, 2002.

"Cole Bombers Identified as Veterans of Afghan War," *Washington Post*, November 17, 2000.

Creel, George, *How We Advertised America*, New York: Arno Press, 1972.

"The Danger Within," *Far Eastern Economic Review*, September 27, 2001.

Darley, J. M., and C. D. Batson, "From Jerusalem to Jericho: A Study of Situational and Dispositional Variables in Helping Behavior," Journal of Personality and Social Psychology, No. 27, 1973, pp. 100–108.

Davis, Paul K., and Brian Michael Jenkins, *Deterrence and Influence in Counterterrorism: A Component in the War on al Qaeda*, Santa Monica, Calif.: RAND Corporation, MR-1619-DARPA, 2002.

Diefendorf, Jeffrey, Axel Frohn, and Hermann Rupieper, eds., *American Policy and the Reconstruction of West Germany, 1945–1955*, New York: Cambridge University Press, 1993.

"Double Whammy: One ID'd in Cole Attack; 5 Indicted for Embassy Bombing," *ABCNews.com*, December 21, 2000.

Drolet, Aimee, and Jennifer Aaker, "Off-Target? Changing Cognitive-Based Attitudes," *Journal of Consumer Research*, Vol. 12, No. 1, 2002, pp. 59–68.

Deutch, M., and H. B. Gerard, "A Study of Normative and Informational Social Influence upon Judgement," *Journal of Abnormal and Social Psychology*, No. 51, 1955, pp. 629–636.

Eagly, A., "Comprehensibility of Persuasive Arguments as a Determinant of Opinion Change," *Journal of Personality and Social Psychology*, No. 29, pp. 758–773.

Eagly, A., and S. Chaiken, *The Psychology of Attitudes*, Fort Worth, Tex.: Harcourt Brace Jovanovich, 1993.

Eagly, A., W. Wood, and S. Chaiken, "Causal Inferences About Communicators and Their Effect on Opinion Change," *Journal of Personality and Social Psychology*, 1978, No. 36, 1978, pp. 424–435.

Esser, J., "Alive and Well After Twenty-Five Years: A Review of Groupthink Research," *Organizational Behavior and Human Decision Processes*, No. 73, 1998, pp. 116–141.

"European Police Focus on North African Links; Diaspora Seen as Pool for Terror Cells," *International Herald Tribune*, September 9, 2002.

Executive Office of the President, "U.S. Counterterrorism Strategy," White House, February 2003.

Falkenrath, Richard, et al., *America's Achilles Heel: Nuclear, Biological, and Chemical Terrorism and Covert Attack*, Cambridge, Mass.: MIT Press, 1998.

Festinger, L., "A Theory of Social Comparison Processes," *Human Relations*, No. 7, 1954, pp. 117–140.

_____, *A Theory of Cognitive Dissonance*, Stanford, Calif.: Stanford University Press, 1957.

Festinger, L., and J. M. Carlsmith, "Cognitive Consequences of Forced Compliance," *Journal of Abnormal and Social Psychology*, No. 58, 203–211.

"Fighting Terror: Clerics May Have Stoked Radicals' Fire," *Boston Globe*, August 4, 2002.

Fishbein, M., M. Goldberg, and S. Middlestadt, *Social Marketing: Theoretical and Practical Perspectives*, Atlanta, Ga.: Lawrence Erlbaum Associates, 1997.

Ford, Peter, "Europe Cringes at President Bush's 'Crusade' Against Terrorism," *Christian Science Monitor*, September 19, 2001.

Freedman, J., and S. Fraser, "Compliance Without Pressure: The Foot-in-the-Door Technique," *Journal of Experimental Psychology*, No. 4, 1966, pp. 195–203.

"From Defender of the Faith to Terrorist: Yemen's Religious Academics," *The Economist*, May 30, 2002.

"German at Center of Sept. 11 Inquiry; Suspect Recruited Hijackers in Hamburg," *Washington Post,* June 12, 2002.

Gerwehr, S., and R. Glenn, *The Art of Darkness,* Santa Monica, Calif.: RAND Corporation, MR-1132-A, 2000.

_____, *Unweaving the Web,* Santa Monica, Calif.: RAND Corporation, MR-1495-A, 2003.

Giles, H., and J. M. Wiemann, "Language, Social Comparison and Power," in Berger and Chaffee (1987, pp. 350–384).

Gonzales, M., E. Aronson, and M. Costanzo, "Increasing the Effectiveness of Energy Auditors: A Field Experiment," *Journal of Applied Social Psychology,* Vol. 18, 1988, pp. 1049–1066.

Greenwald, Anthony, and Albert Rosita, "Acceptance and Recall of Improvised Arguments," *Journal of Personality and Social Psychology,* No. 8, 1968, pp. 31–34.

Gunaratna, Rohan, *Inside Al-Qaeda: Global Network of Terror,* New York: Columbia University Press, 2002.

Guetzkow, H., ed., *Groups, Leadership, and Men,* Pittsburgh, Pa.: Carnegie Press, 1951.

Hales, Robert, Stuart Yudofsky, and John Talbott, eds., *Textbook of Psychiatry,* 3rd edition, Washington, D.C.: American Psychiatric Press, 1999.

"Hambali 'Eyed Bangkok Embassies'," *BBC News Online Edition,* August 22, 2003.

Hass, R., "Effects of Source Characteristics on Cognitive Responses and Persuasion," in Petty, Ostrom, and Brock (1981).

Head, William, and Lawrence Grinter, eds., *Looking Back on the Vietnam War: A 1990s Perspective on the Decisions, Combat and Legacies,* Westport, Conn.: Greenwood Publishing Group, 1993.

Herek, G., I. Janis, and P. Huth, "Decision-Making During International Crises: Is Quality of Process Related to Outcome?" *Journal of Conflict Resolution,* Vol. 31, No. 2, pp. 203–226.

Hoffman, Bruce, *Inside Terrorism,* New York: Colombia University Press, 1998.

Hosmer, Stephen T., *Psychological Effects of U.S. Air Operations in Four Wars 1941–1991: Lessons for U.S. Commanders*, Santa Monica, Calif.: RAND Corporation, MR-576-AF, 1996.

"Hostage to Fortune and Yemeni Guns," *The Guardian*, December 30, 1998.

Hovland, C., and W. Weiss, "The Influence of Source Credibility on Communication Effectiveness," *Public Opinion Quarterly*, No. 15, 1951, pp. 635–650.

Hovland, Carl I., Irving Janis, and Harold Kelley, *Communication and Persuasion*, New Haven: Yale University Press, 1953.

Hovland, C. I., A. Lumsdaine, and F. Sheffield, *Experiments on Mass Communication*, Princeton, N.J.: Princeton University Press, 1949.

"Impact of the Bali Bombings," International Crisis Group Report, Jakarta/Brussels, October 24, 2002.

"Indonesia: Violence and Radical Muslims," International Crisis Group Indonesia Briefing Paper, October 10, 2001.

Insko, C., R. Smith, M. Alicke, J. Wade, and S. Taylor, "Conformity and Group Size: The Concern with Being Right and the Concern with Being Liked," *Personality and Social Psychology*, No. 11, 1985, pp. 41–50.

"Is Yemen a Conduit for Global Terrorism?" *Christian Science Monitor*, March 31, 2000.

Isenberg, D., "Group Polarization: A Critical Review and Meta Analysis," *Journal of Personality and Social Psychology*, Vol. 50, No. 6, 1986, pp. 1141–1151.

Janis, Irving, *Victims of Groupthink*, Boston: Houghton Mifflin, 1972.

_____, *Groupthink: Psychological Studies of Policy Decisions and Fiascoes*, Boston: Houghton Mifflin, 1982.

Johnson, A. R., "Winning Hearts and Minds: Cold War Victories and Post 9/11 Challenges," *Hoover Digest*, Fall 2003.

Kellen, K., *Conversations with Enemy Soldiers in Late 1968/Early 1969: A Study of Motivation and Morale*, Santa Monica, Calif.: RAND Corporation, RM-6131-1-ISA/ARPA, 1970.

Kepel, Gilles, *Allah in the West: Islamic Movements in America and Europe*, Susan Milner, trans., Stanford, Calif.: Stanford University Press, 1997.

_____, *Jihad: The Trail of Political Islam*, London: I. B. Tauris, 2002.

Kerchner, P., R. Deckro, and J. Kloeber, "Valuing Psychological Operations," *Military Operations Research*, Vol. 6, No. 2, 2001, pp. 45–65.

Koch, J. A., *The Chieu Hoi Program in South Vietnam, 1963–1971*, Santa Monica, Calif.: RAND Corporation, R-1172-ARPA, 1973.

Kurzman, Charles, *Liberal Islam*, New York: Oxford University Press, 1998.

Lackey, Sue, "Yemen: Unlikely Key to Western Security," *Jane's Intelligence Review*, October 12, 2000.

Lasswell, Harold, "The Structure and Function of Communication in Society," in Bryson (1948).

Lifton, Robert J., *Thought Reform and the Psychology of Totalism*, New York: Norton, 1969.

Lindzey, G., and E. Aronson, eds., *Handbook of Social Psychology* (Volume 2), New York: McGraw-Hill, 1985.

Lippman, Walter, *Public Opinion*, New York: Harcourt-Brace, 1922.

Lord, C., L. Ross, and M. Lepper, "Biased Assimilation and Attitude Polarization," *Journal of Personality and Social Psychology*, No. 37, 1979, pp. 2098–2109.

Luehrsen, Kenneth, and Virginia Walbot, "Firefly Luciferase as a Reporter for Plant Gene Expression Studies," *Promega Notes*, No. 44, 1993, p. 24.

Mackintosh-Smith, Tim, *Yemen: The Unknown Arabia*, New York: Overlook Press, 2000.

"Man Alleged to Aid 9/11 Cell Arrested in German Inquiry: Moroccan Man Assisted Hamburg Group, Officials Say," *Washington Post*, October 11, 2002.

Maslach, C., J. Stapp, and R. Santee, "Individuation," *Journal of Personality and Social Psychology*, No. 49, pp. 729–738.

McAlister, Leigh, and Michael L. Rothschild, eds., *Advances in Consumer Research*, Provo, Utah: Association for Consumer Research, 1993.

McCormick, Gordan, *The Shining Path and the Future of Peru*, Santa Monica, Calif.: RAND Corporation, R-3781-DOS/OSD, 1990.

_____, *From the Sierra to the Cities: The Urban Campaign of the Shining Path*, Santa Monica, Calif.: RAND Corporation, R-4150-USDP, 1992.

McGuire, W. J., "Inducing Resistance to Persuasion," in L. Berkowitz (1964, pp. 191–229).

_____, "Personality and Susceptibility to Social Influence," in Borgatta and Lambert (1968, pp. 1130–1187).

McInnis, Edgar, Richard Hiscocks, and Robert Spencer, *The Shaping of Postwar Germany*, New York: Praeger, 1960.

McLaurin, R. D., *The Battle of Sidon*, Aberdeen Proving Ground, Md.: U.S. Army Human Engineering Laboratories, 1989.

Milgram, S., *Obedience to Authority*, New York: Harper & Row, 1974.

_____, *Obedience to Authority: An Experimental View*, New York: Harper-Collins, 1983.

Mitchell, Andrew, *Advertising Exposure, Memory, and Choice*, 9th edition, Hillsdale, N.J.: Lawrence Erlbaum Associates, 1990.

Moscovici, S., "Social Influence and Conformity," in Lindzey and Aronson (1985).

Myers, D., and H. Lamm, "The Group Polarization Phenomenon," *Psychological Bulletin*, No. 83, 1975, pp. 602–627.

Newport, Frank, ed., *The 2002 Gallup Poll of the Islamic World: Tuesday Briefing*, Princeton, N.J.: The Gallup Organization, February 2002.

"No Connections: Bin Laden Denies Link to Cole Blast, Kuwait Plot," *CNN.com*, November 13, 2000.

Office of the Press Secretary, "President Discusses the Future of Iraq," February 26, 2003.

O'Neill, Bard, *Terrorism and Insurgency,* Washington, D.C.: Brassey's, 1998.

"One Sheik's Mission: To Teach the Young to Despise Western Culture," *New York Times*, December 17, 2000.

"Orders from Osama; Sources: Cole Suspect Believes Orders Came from bin Laden," *ABCNews.com*, January 8, 2001.

Page, C., *U.S. Official Propaganda During the Vietnam War: 1965–1973*, London: Leicester University Press, 1996.

Pascall, B., and S. White, *Eliminating Violence in Hockey*, Vancouver, B.C.: Ministry of Small Business, Tourism, and Culture, 2000.

Petty R., and J. Cacioppo, *Attitudes and Persuasion: Classic and Contemporary Approaches*, Dubuque, Iowa: Wm. C. Brown, 1981.

_____, *Communication and Persuasion: Central and Peripheral Routes to Attitude Change*, New York: Springer-Verlag, 1986.

Petty, R. E., T. M. Ostrom, and T. C. Brock, eds., *Responses in Persuasion*, Hillsdale, N.J.: Lawrence Erlbaum Associates, 1981.

Pye, L., *Observations on the Chieu Hoi Program*, Santa Monica, Calif.: RAND Corporation, RM-4864-1-ARPA, 1969.

Riche, M., "Psychographics for the 1990s," *American Demographics*, July 1989, pp. 24–55.

Rink, Steffen, "Under the Banner of Dialogue and Transparency: Mosques in Germany," Goethe Institute, n.d., www.goethe.de/kug/ges/rel/thm/en30158.htm (accessed October 2004).

Rohrer, J., S. Baron, E. Hoffman, and D. Swander, "The Stability of Auto-kinetic Judgments," *Journal of Abnormal and Social Psychology*, No. 49, pp. 595–559.

"Rooting Out Their Radicals: Saudi Arabia, Kuwait, and Yemen Have to Admit That All Is Not As It Should Be," *The Economist*, November 21, 2002.

Roloff, M. E., and G. R. Miller, eds., *Interpersonal Processes: New Directions in Communication Research*, Newbury Park, Calif.: Sage Publications, 1987.

Russo, A., "Comments on the Development and Implementation of a Chieu Hoi Appeal Designed to Attract Viet Cong Cadre," Santa Monica, Calif.: RAND Corporation, D-15661-ARPA/AGILE/IS, 1967.

Sakarai, M., "Small Group Cohesiveness and Detrimental Conformity," *Sociometry*, No. 38, pp. 340–357.

Saunders, F., *The Cultural Cold War: The CIA and the World of Arts and Letters*, New York: The New Press, 2001.

Schein, E., *Coercive Persuasion*, New York: Norton, 1961.

Schreiber, S. C., "Psychiatric Interview, Psychiatric History and Mental Status Exam," in Hales, Yudofsky, and Talbott (1999, pp. 193–223).

Schuman, H., and S. Presser, *Questions and Answers in Attitude Surveys: Experiments on Question Form, Wording and Context*, Orlando, Fla.: Academic Press, 1981.

Schumann, D., R. Petty, and D. Clemons, "Predicting the Effectiveness of Different Strategies of Advertising Variation," *Journal of Consumer Research*, No. 17, 1990, pp. 192–202.

Schwartz, Thomas A., *America's Germany*, Cambridge, Mass.: Harvard University Press, 1991.

Schwarzwald, J., A. Bizman, and M. Raz, "The Foot-in-the-Door Paradigm: Effects of Second Request Size on Donation Probability and Donor Generosity," *Personality and Social Psychology Bulletin*, No. 9, 1983, pp. 443–450.

Sherif, M., and C. L. Hovland, *Social Judgment: Assimilation and Contrast Effects in Communication and Attitude Change,* New Haven, Conn.: Yale University Press, 1961.

Short, K., ed., *Broadcasting Over the Iron Curtain*, New York: St. Martin's Press, 1986.

Simpson, Christopher, *Science of Coercion: Communication Research and Psychological Warfare 1945–1960*, New York: Oxford University Press, 1994.

Skilling, H. G., *Samizdat and an Independent Society in Central and Eastern Europe*, Columbus, Ohio: Ohio State University Press, 1989.

Smucker, Philip, "Where Holy Warriors Learn the Fundamentals," *Christian Science Monitor*, February 6, 2001.

Snyder, M., and M. R. Cunningham, "To Comply or Not to Comply: Testing the Self-Perception Explanation of the Foot in the Door Phenomenon," *Journal of Personality and Social Psychology*, No. 31, 1975, pp. 64–67.

Soley, L., *Radio Warfare: OSS and CIA Subversive Propaganda*, Westport, Conn.: Praeger, 1989.

"Storm Clouds on the Horizon," *Far Eastern Economic Review*, February 14, 2002.

Taylor, P., *Munitions of the Mind*, Manchester, UK: Manchester University Press, 1995.

Tesser, A., "Self-Generated Attitude Change," in Berkowitz (1978).

Tesser, A., and M. Conlee, "Some Effects of Time and Thought on Attitude Polarization," *Journal of Personality and Social Psychology*, No. 31, 1975, pp. 262–270.

Tetlock, P., R. Peterson, C. Mcguire, S. Chang, and P. Feld, "Assessing Political Group Dynamics: A Test of the Groupthink Model," *Journal of Personality and Social Psychology*, Vol. 63, No. 3, pp. 403–425.

"Threats and Responses: Arrests in Europe; Franks Links Tunisian in Jail to Terror Cells in 5 Nations," *New York Times*, October 23, 2002.

"To Mollify Iraqis, US Plans to Ease Scope of Its Raids," *New York Times*, August 7, 2003.

"Traces of Terror: Sept. 11 Attack Planned in '99, Germans Learn," *New York Times*, August 30, 2002.

"Traces of Terror: The Terror Trail: German Officials Deny Knowing Whereabouts of Important Figure in Hamburg Plot," *New York Times*, June 13, 2002.

Uleman, J. S., and J. A. Bargh, eds., *Unintended Thought*, New York: Guilford Press, 1989.

U.S. Department of State, "Fact Sheet: State Dept. Updates List of Terrorist Individuals and Groups," October 11, 2002.

U.S. Joint Chiefs of Staff, *Joint Doctrine for Psychological Operations*, Joint Publication 3-53, 1996.

_____, *Department of Defense Dictionary of Military and Associated Terms*, Joint Publication 1-02, 2004.

"U.S.: Top al Qaeda Operative Arrested," *CNN.com*, November 22, 2002.

"USS Cole Suspect Involved in US Embassy Blast in Nairobi," *Yemen Times*, November 20, 2000.

Wastell, David, "Bush Speech Crafted to Unify Hawks and Doves in Cabinet," *Telegraph.co.uk*, September 23, 2001.

"Weak Link in the Anti-Terror Chain," *Far Eastern Economic Review*, October 24, 2004.

Weiss, M., *The Clustering of America*, New York: Harper & Row, 1988.

"What If He Isn't Guilty?" *Far Eastern Economic Review,* November 7, 2002.

"Yemen: Coping with Terrorism and Violence in a Fragile State," *International Crisis Group Report,* January 2003.

"Yemen: Unlikely Key to Western Security," *Jane's Intelligence Review,* October 12, 2000.

"Yemen Feels the Backlash," *Jane's Defence Weekly,* Vol. 38, No. 16, October 16, 2002.

"Yemen Quakes in Cole's Shadow," *Christian Science Monitor,* September 21, 2001.

Zanna, M., "Message Receptivity: A New Look at the Old Problem of Open- vs. Closed-Mindedness," in Mitchell (1990).

Zanna, M. P., J. M. Olson, and C. P. Herman, eds., *Social Influence: The Ontario Symposium,* Hillsdale, N.J.: Lawrence Erlbaum Associates, 1987.

Ziemke, W., *The US Army in the Occupation of Germany 1944–1946,* Washington, D.C.: Center of Military History, 1975.

Zimbardo, P., and M. Leippe, *The Psychology of Attitude Change and Social Influence,* Boston: McGraw-Hill, 1991.

Zogby, James J., *What Arabs Think: Values, Beliefs, and Concerns,* Washington, D.C.: Zogby International, September 2002.

Additional References

Ajzen, I., "From Intentions to Actions: A Theory of Planned Behavior," in J. Kuhl and J. Beckmann, eds., *Action-Control: From Cognition to Behavior,* Heidelberg, Germany: Springer-Verlag, 1985, pp. 11–39.

Allison, S. T., and D. M. Messick, "The Group Attribution Error," *Journal of Experimental Social Psychology,* No. 21, 1985, pp. 563–579.

Allport, G., *Institutional Behavior,* Chapel Hill, N.C.: University of North Carolina Press, 1933.

_____, *The Nature of Prejudice,* Reading, Mass.: Addison-Wesley, 1954.

Altman, I., and D. A. Taylor, *Social Penetration,* New York: Holst, Rinehart, Winston, 1973.

Anderson, C., "Abstract and Concrete Data in the Perseverance of Social Theories: When Weak Data Lead to Unshakable Beliefs," *Journal of Experimental Social Psychology*, No. 19, 1983, pp. 93–108.

Anderson, C., M. Lepper, and L. Ross, "Perseverance of Social Theories: The Role of Explanation in the Persistence of Discredited Information," *Journal of Personality and Social Psychology*, No. 39, 1980, pp. 1037–1049.

Arkes, H., and C. Blumer, "The Psychology of Sunk Cost," *Organizational Behavior and Human Decision Processes*, No. 35, 1985, pp. 124–140.

Arkes, H., L. Boehm, and G. Xu, "Determinants of Judged Validity," *Journal of Experimental Social Psychology*, No. 27, 1991, pp. 576–605.

Aronson, E., and B. Golden, "The Effect of Relevant and Irrelevant Aspects of Communicator Credibility on Opinion Change," *Journal of Personality*, No. 30, 1962, pp. 135–146.

Aronson, E., and J. Mills, "The Effect of Severity of Initiation on Liking for a Group," *Journal of Abnormal and Social Psychology*, No. 59, 1959, pp. 177–181.

Aronson, E., and J. M. Carlsmith, "Effects of Severity of Threat in the Devaluation of Forbidden Behavior," *Journal of Abnormal and Social Psychology*, No. 66, 1963, pp. 584–588.

Asch, S. E., "Forming Impressions of Personality," *Journal of Abnormal and Social Psychology*, No. 41, 1946, pp. 258–290.

_____, "Opinions and Social Pressure," in A. P. Hare, E. F. Borgatta, and R. F. Bales, eds., *Small Groups: Studies in Social Interaction*, New York: Alfred A. Knopf, 1966, pp. 318–324.

Bandura, A., *Social Learning Theory*, New York: General Learning Press, 1971.

_____, *Social Foundations of Thought and Action*, Engelwood Cliffs, N.J.: Prentice-Hall, 1986.

Baron, R. A., and D. Byrne, *Social Psychology*, 8th edition, Boston: Allyn and Bacon, 1997.

Batson, C. D., *The Altruism Question: Towards a Social Social-Psychological Answer*, Hillsdale, N.J.: Lawrence Erlbaum Associates, 1991.

Baxter, T. L., and L. R. Goldberg, "Perceived Behavioral Inconsistency Underlying Trait Attributions to Oneself and Another: An Extension of the Actor-Observer Effect," *Personality and Social Psychology Bulletin*, No. 13, 1988, pp. 437–447.

Bell, D. E., "Regret in Decision Making Under Uncertainty," *Operations Research*, No. 30, 1982, pp. 961–981.

Bem, D. J., "Self-Perception Theory," in L. Berkowitz, ed., *Advances in Experimental Social Psychology*, Vol. 6, New York: Academic Press, 1972, pp. 1–62.

Berger, C. R., "Beyond Initial Interaction: Uncertainty, Understanding and the Development of Interpersonal Relationships," in H. Giles and R. St. Clair, eds., *Language and Social Psychology*, Oxford: Basil Blackwell, 1979.

Berger, C. R., and R. J. Calabrese, "Some Explorations in Initial Interaction and Beyond: Toward a Developmental Theory of Interpersonal Communication," *Human Communication Research*, No. 1, 1975, pp. 99–112.

Berger, C. R., and W. B. Gudykunst, "Uncertainty and Communication," in B. Dervin and M. Voight, eds., *Progress in Communication Sciences*, Norwood, N.J.: Ablex, 1991.

Berger, P. L., and T. Luckmann, *The Social Construction of Reality*, Garden City, N.Y.: Doubleday, 1967.

Berkowitz, L., and J. Green, "The Stimulus Qualities of the Scapegoat," *Journal of Abnormal and Social Psychology*, No. 7, 1962, pp. 202–207.

Berscheid, E., W. Graziano, T. Monson, and M. Dermer, "Outcome Dependency: Attention, Attribution, and Attraction," *Journal of Personality and Social Psychology*, No. 34, 1976, pp. 978–989.

Blaney, P., "Affect and Memory: A Review," *Psychological Bulletin*, No. 99, 1986, pp. 229–246.

Bodenhausen, G. V., "Stereotypic Biases in Social Decision Making and Memory: Testing Process Models of Stereotype Use," *Journal of Personality and Social Psychology*, No. 55, 1988, pp. 726–737.

Bower, G. H., "Mood and Memory," *American Psychologist*, No. 36, 1981, pp. 129–148.

Brehm, J., and A. Cohen, *Explorations in Cognitive Dissonance*, New York: Wiley, 1962.

Brehm, J. W., "Postdecision Changes in the Desirability of Alternatives," *Journal of Abnormal and Social Psychology*, No. 52, 1956, pp. 384–389.

Brown, P., and S. Levinson, "Universals in Language Usage: Politeness Phenomena," in E. N. Goody, ed., *Questions and Politeness: Strategies in Social Interaction*, New York: Cambridge University Press, 1978, pp. 56–289.

Bruner, J., and R. Taguiri, "Person Perception," in G. Lindzey, ed., *Handbook of Social Psychology*, Vol. 2, Reading, Mass.: Addison Wesley, 1954.

Brunstein, J. C., and P. M. Gollwitzer, "Effects of Failure on Subsequent Performance: The Importance of Self-Defining Goals," *Journal of Personality and Social Psychology*, No. 70, 1996, pp. 395–407.

Buller, D. B., and J. K. Burgoon, "Deception: Strategic and Nonstrategic Communication," in J. A. Daly and J. M. Wiemann, eds., *Strategic Interpersonal Communication*, Hillsdale, N.J.: Lawrence Erlbaum Associates, 1994, pp. 191–223.

_____, "Interpersonal Deception Theory," *Communication Theory*, Vol. 6, No. 3, 1996, pp. 203–242.

Buller, D. B., K. D. Strzyzewski, and J. Comstock, "Interpersonal Deception: I. Deceivers' Reactions to Receivers' Suspicions and Probing," *Communications Monographs*, No. 58, 1991, pp. 1–24.

Burgoon, J. K., "A Communications Model of Personal Space Violations: Explications and an Initial Test," *Human Communications Research*, No. 4, 1978, pp. 129–142.

Burgoon, J. K., and , D. B. Buller, "Interpersonal Deception: IV. Effects of Deceit on Perceived Communication and Nonverbal Behavior Dynamics," *Journal of Nonverbal Behavior*, No. 18, 1994, pp. 155–184.

Burgoon, J. K., and J. L. Hale, "Nonverbal Expectancy Violations: Model Elaboration and Application to Immediacy Behaviors," *Communication Monographs*, No. 51, 1988, pp. 193–214.

Burgoon, J. K., and B. A. Le Poire, "Effects of Communication Expectancies, Actual Communication and Expectancy Disconfirmation on Evaluations of Communicators and Their Communication Behavior," *Human Communications Research*, No. 20, 1993, pp. 75–105.

Burgoon, J. K., D. B. Buller, and W. G. Woodall, *Nonverbal Communication*, New York: McGraw-Hill, 1996.

Burgoon, M., "The Effects of Message Variables on Opinion and Attitude Change," in J. Bradac, ed., *Messages in Communication Sciences: Contemporary Approaches to the Study of Effects,* Newbury Park, Calif.: Sage Publications, 1989, pp. 129–164.

_____, "Language Expectancy Theory: Elaboration, Explication and Extension," in C. R. Berger and M. Burgoon, eds., *Communication and Social Influence Processes* , East Lansing, Mich.: Michigan State University Press, 1995, pp. 29–51.

Burgoon, M., S. Jones, and D. Stewart, "Towards a Message-Centered Theory of Persuasion: Three Empirical Investigations of Language Intensity," *Human Communications Research*, No. 1, 1975, pp. 240–256.

Burnstein, E., and Y. Schul, "The Informational Basis of Social Judgments: Operations in Forming an Impression of Another Person," *Journal of Experimental Social Psychology*, No. 18, 1982, pp. 217–234.

Byrne, D., and G. L. Clore, "A Reinforcement Model of Evaluative Processes," *Personality: An International Journal*, No. 1, 1970, pp. 103–128.

Cacioppo, J., R. Petty, and J. Sidera, "The Effects of a Salient Self-Schema on the Evaluation of Proattitudinal Editorials: Top-Down Versus Bottom-Up Message Processing," *Journal of Experimental Social Psychology*, No. 18, 1982, pp. 324–338.

Chaiken, S., W. Wood, and A. H. Eagly, "Principles of Persuasion," in E. T. Higgins and A. Kruglanski, eds., *Social Psychology: Handbook of Basic Mechanisms and Processes*, New York: Guilford Press, 1996.

Chapman, L. J., "Illusory Correlation in Observational Report," *Journal of Verbal Learning and Verbal Behavior*, No. 5, 1967, pp. 151–155.

Chess, C., M. Tamuz, A. Saville, and M. Greenberg, "Reducing Uncertainty and Increasing Credibility," *Industrial Crisis Quarterly*, No. 6, 1992, pp. 55–70.

Cialdini, R., *Influence: Science and Practice*, 3rd edition, New York: HarperCollins, 1993.

Clark, R. A., and J. G. Delia, "The Development of Functional Persuasive Skills in Childhood and Early Adolescence," *Child Development*, No. 47, 1976, pp. 1008–1014.

Cohen, C. E., "Person Categories and Social Perception: Testing Some Boundary Conditions of the Processing Effects of Prior Knowledge," *Journal of Personality and Social Psychology*, No. 40, 1981, pp. 441–452.

Covello, V., and F. Allen, *Seven Cardinal Rules of Risk Communication*, U.S. Environmental Protection Agency: Office of Policy Analysis, 1988.

Creel, G., *How We Advertised America*, New York: Arno Press, 1972.

Daugherty, W., and M. Janowitz, eds., *A Psychological Warfare Casebook*, Baltimore, Md.: Johns Hopkins University Press, 1958.

Dawes, R. M., and M. Mulford, "The False Consensus Effect and Overconfidence: Flaws in Judgment, or Flaws in How We Study Judgment?" *Organizational Behavior and Human Decision Processes*, No. 65, 1996, pp. 201–211.

Deci, E. L., *Intrinsic Motivation*, New York: Plenum Press, 1975.

Delia, J. G., and W. H. Crockett, "Social Schemas, Cognitive Complexity and the Learning of Social Structures," *Journal of Personality*, No. 41, 1973, pp. 413–429.

Diener, E., S. C. Fraser, A. L. Beaman, and R. T. Kelem, "Effects of Deindividuation Variables on Stealing Among Halloween Trick-or-Treaters," *Journal of Personality and Social Psychology*, Vol. 33, No. 2, 1976, pp. 178–183.

Downes-Le Guin, T., and B. Hoffman, *The Impact of Terrorism on Public Opinion, 1988 to 1989*, Santa Monica, Calif.: RAND Corporation, 1993.

Eagly, A., *Sex Differences in Social Behavior: A Social-Role Interpretation*, Hillsdale, N.J.: Lawrence Erlbaum Associate, 1987.

Eagly, A., and S. Chaiken, "Attitude Structure and Function," in D. T. Gilbert, S. T. Fiske, and G. Lindzey, eds., *The Handbook of Social Psychology*, Vol. 1, 4th edition, New York: McGraw-Hill, 1998, pp. 269–322.

Einhorn, H. J., and R. M. Hogarth, "Behavioral Decision Theory: Processes of Judgment and Choice," *Annual Review of Psychology*, No. 32, 1981, pp. 53–88.

Fein, S., and J. Hilton, "Judging Others in the Shadow of Suspicion," *Motivation and Emotion*, No. 18, 1994, pp. 167–198.

Fein, S., J. Hilton, and D. Miller, "Suspicion of Ulterior Motivation and Correspondence Bias," *Journal of Personality and Social Psychology,* No. 58, 1990, pp. 753–764.

Festinger, L., and J. M. Carlsmith, "Cognitive Consequences of Forced Compliance," *Journal of Abnormal and Social Psychology,* No. 58, 1959, pp. 203–211.

Festinger, L., S. Schachter, and K. W. Back, *Social Pressures in Informal Groups: A Study of Human Factors in Housing,* New York: Harper, 1950.

Festinger, L., A. Pepitone, and T. Newcomb, "Some Consequences of Deindividuation in a Group," *Journal of Abnormal and Social Psychology,* No. 47, 1952, pp. 382–389.

Fischhoff, B., P. Slovic, and S. Lichtenstein, "Knowing with Certainty: The Appropriateness of Extreme Confidence," *Journal of Experimental Psychology: Human Perception and Performance,* No. 3, 1977, pp. 552–564.

Fishbein, M., and I. Ajzen, *Belief, Attitude, Intention and Behavior: An Introduction to Theory and Research,* Reading, Mass.: Addison-Wesley, 1975.

Fishbein, M., M. Goldberg, and S. Middlestadt, *Social Marketing: Theoretical and Practical Perspectives,* Atlanta, Ga.: Lawrence Erlbaum Associates, 1997.

Fisher, R. J., "Social Desirability Bias and the Validity of Indirect Questioning," *Journal of Consumer Research,* No. 20, 1993, pp. 303–315.

Fiske, S. T., and S. E. Taylor, *Social Cognition,* 2nd edition, New York: McGraw-Hill, 1991.

Forgas, J. P., "Mood and Judgment: The Affect Infusion Model (AIM)," *Psychological Bulletin,* No. 117, 1995, pp. 39–66.

French, J. P. R. Jr., and B. Raven, "The Bases of Social Power," in D. Cartwright and A. Zander, eds., *Group Dynamics,* New York: Harper and Row, 1960, pp. 607–623.

Frijda, N., *The Emotions: Studies in Emotion and Social Interaction,* New York: Cambridge University Press, 1986.

Furnam, A., "The Robustness of the Recency Effect: Studies Using Legal Evidence," *The Journal of General Psychology,* Vol. 113, No. 4, 1986, pp. 351–357.

Gass, R. H., and J. S. Seiter, *Persuasion, Social Influence, and Compliance Gaining*, Needham Heights, Mass.: Allyn and Bacon, 1999.

Gemmill, G., "The Dynamics of Scapegoating in Small Groups," *Small Group Behavior*, No. 20, 1998, pp. 406–418.

George, A., "The Case for Multiple Advocacy in Making Foreign Policy," *American Political Science Review*, No. 66, 1972.

_____, "The Role of Knowledge in Policy-Making," in *Bridging the Gap: Theory and Practice in Foreign Policy*, Washington, D.C.: U.S. Institute of Peace, 1993.

Gilbert, D. T., and P. S. Malone, "The Correspondence Bias," *Psychological Bulletin*, No. 117, 1995, pp. 21–38.

Gilbert, D. T., R. W. Tafarodi, and P. S. Malone, "You Can't Not Believe Everything You Read," *Journal of Personality and Social Psychology*, No. 65, pp. 221–233.

Glasser, W., *Control Theory: A New Explanation of How We Control Our Lives*, New York, Harper and Row, 1984.

Goldstein, F., *Psychological Operations: Principles and Case Studies*, Maxwell AFB, Alab.: Air University Press, 1996.

Gollwitzer, P. M., and R. A. Wicklund, "Self-Symbolizing and the Neglect of Others' Perspectives," *Journal of Personality and Social Psychology*, No. 48, 1985, pp. 702–715.

Guttman, L., "A Basis for Scaling Qualitative Data," *American Sociological Review*, No. 9, 1944, pp. 139–150.

Hamill, R., T. D. Wilson, and R. E. Nisbett, "Insensitivity to Sample Bias: Generalizing from Atypical Cases," *Journal of Personality and Social Psychology*, No. 39, 1980, pp. 578–589.

Hamilton, D., ed., *Cognitive Processes in Stereotyping and Intergroup Behavior*, Hillsdale, N.J.: Lawrence Erlbaum Associates, 1981.

Hamilton, D., and T. Rose, "Illusory Correlation and the Maintenance of Stereotypical Beliefs," *Journal of Personality and Social Psychology*, No. 39, 1980, pp. 832–845.

Hass, R., and K. Grady, "Temporal Delay, Type of Warning, and Resistance to Influence," *Journal of Experimental Social Psychology*, No. 11, 1975, pp. 459–469.

Heider, F., *The Psychology of Interpersonal Relations*, New York: Wiley, 1958.

Hewstone, M., *Causal Attribution: From Cognitive Processes to Cognitive Beliefs*, Oxford: Blackwell Publishing, 1989.

Hilton, J., S. Fein, and D. Miller, "Suspicion and Dispositional Inference," *Personality and Social Psychology Bulletin*, No. 19, 1993, pp. 501–512.

Hilton, J. L., and S. Fein, "The Role of Diagnosticity in Stereotype-Based Judgments," *Journal of Personality and Social Psychology*, No. 57, 1989, pp. 201–211.

Hoffman, B., *Inside Terrorism*, New York: Columbia University Press, 1999.

Hogarth, R., *Judgment and Choice*, 2nd edition, New York: Wiley, 1987.

Homans, G. C., *Social Behavior*, New York: Harcourt Brace and World, 1961.

Hovland, C. I., I. L. Janis, and H. H. Kelley, *Communications and Persuasion: Psychological Studies in Opinion Change*, New Haven, Conn.: Yale University Press, 1953.

Hovland, C., and I. Janis, *Personality and Persuasibility*, New Haven: Yale University Press, 1959.

Jackson, J. W., "Realistic Group Conflict Theory: A Review and Evaluation of the Theoretical and Empirical Literature," *Psychological Record*, No. 43, 1993, pp. 395–413.

Janis, I., "Crucial Decisions: Leadership in Policy-Making and Management," New York: Free Press, 1989.

Janis, I., and L. Mann, *Decisionmaking: A Psychological Analysis of Conflict, Choice, and Commitment*, New York: Free Press, 1977.

Jecker, J., and D. Landy, "Liking a Person as Function of Doing Him a Favor," *Human Relations*, No. 22, 1969, pp. 371–378.

Johnson, M. K., S. Hashtroudi, and D. S. Lindsay, "Source Monitoring," *Psychological Bulletin*, No. 114, 1993, pp. 3–28.

Jones, E. E., and K. E. Davis, "From Acts to Dispositions: The Attribution Process in Social Psychology," in L. Berkowitz, ed., *Advances in Experimental Social Psychology*, Vol. 2, New York: Academic Press, 1965, pp. 219–266.

Jones, E. E., and V. A. Harris, "The Attribution of Attitudes," *Journal of Experimental Social Psychology*, No. 3, 1967, pp. 1–24.

Jones, E. E., and R. E. Nisbett, "The Actor and the Observer: Divergent Perceptions of the Causes of the Behavior," in E. E. Jones, D. E. Kanouse, H. H. Kelley, R. E. Nisbett, S. Valins, and B. Weiner, eds., *Attribution: Perceiving the Causes of Behavior*, Morristown, N.J.: General Learning Press, 1972, pp. 79–94.

Jones, M. B., and D. R. Jones, "Preferred Pathways of Behavioral Contagion," *Journal of Psychiatric Research*, No. 29, 1995, pp. 193–209.

Jowett, G., and V. O'Donnell, *Propaganda and Persuasion*, New York: Sage Publications, 1999.

Judd, C., and B. Park, "Out-Group Homogeneity: Judgments of Variability at the Individual and Group Levels," *Journal of Personality and Social Psychology*, No. 54, 1988, pp. 778–788.

Kahneman, D., and D. Miller, "Norm Theory: Comparing Reality to Its Alternatives," *Psychological Review*, No. 80, 1986, pp. 136–153.

Kahneman, D., and A. Tversky, "On the Psychology of Prediction," *Psychology Review*, No. 80, 1973, pp. 237–251.

_____, "The Simulation Heuristic," in D. Kahneman, P. Slovic, and A. Tversky, eds., *Judgment Under Uncertainty: Heuristics and Biases*, New York: Cambridge University Press, 1982, pp. 201–208.

_____, "Choices, Values, Frames," *American Psychologist*, Vol. 39, No. 4, 1983, pp. 341–350.

Kallgren, C., and W. Wood, "Access to Attitude-Relevant Information in Memory as a Determinant of Attitude-Behavior Consistency," *Journal of Experimental Social Psychology*, No. 22, 1986, pp. 328–338.

Karau, S. J., and K. D. Williams, "Social Loafing: A Meta-Analytic Review and Theoretical Integration," *Journal of Personality and Social Psychology*, No. 65, 1993, pp. 681–706.

Kassin, S., and K. Keichel, "The Social Psychology of False Confessions: Compliance, Internalization, and Confabulation," *Psychological Science*, No. 7, 1996, pp. 125–128.

Katz, P., *Communicating with the Vietnamese Through Leaflets*, Saigon: JUSPAO, 1968.

Kelley, H., "The Processes of Causal Attribution," *American Psychologist,* No. 28, 1973, pp. 107–128.

Kelley, H. H., "Attribution Theory in Social Psychology," in D. Levine, ed., *Nebraska Symposium on Motivation,* Vol. 15, Lincoln, Neb.: University of Nebraska Press, 1967, pp. 192–238.

_____, "Attribution in Social Interaction," in E. E. Jones, D. E. Kanouse, H. H. Kelley, R. E. Nisbett, S. Valins, and B. Weiner, eds., *Attribution: Perceiving the Causes of Behavior,* Morristown, N.J.: General Learning Press, 1972, pp. 1–26.

Kelley, H. H., and J. Thibaut, *Interpersonal Relations: A Theory of Interdependence,* New York: Wiley, 1978.

King, P., and K. Kitchener, *Developing Reflective Judgement: Understanding and Promoting Intellectual Growth and Critical Thinking in Adolescents and Adults,* San Francisco: Jossey-Bass, 1994.

Klayman, J., and Y. W. Ha, "Confirmation, Disconfirmation, and Information in Hypothesis Testing," *Psychological Review,* No. 94, 1987, pp. 211–228.

Knox, R., and J. Inkster, "Postdecision Dissonance at Post Time," *Journal of Personality and Social Psychology,* No. 8, 1968, pp. 319–323.

Koehler, D., "Explanation, Imagination, and Confidence in Judgment," *Psychological Bulletin,* No. 110, 1991, pp. 499–519.

Kruglanski, A., "Motivation Effects in the Social Comparison of Opinions," *Journal of Personality and Social Psychology,* No. 53, 1987, pp. 834–842.

Kruglanski, A. W., and D. M. Webster, "Motivated Closing of the Mind: 'Seizing' and 'Freezing'," *Psychological Review,* No. 103, 1996, pp. 263–283.

Kunda, Z., and R. E. Nisbett, "Prediction and the Partial Understanding of the Law of Large Numbers," *Journal of Experimental Social Psychology,* No. 22, 1986, pp. 339–354.

Lasswell, H., *Propaganda Technique in World War I,* Cambridge, Mass.: MIT Press, 1971.

Latané, B., "The Psychology of Social Impact," *American Psychologist,* No. 36, 1981, pp. 343–356.

Latané, B., and J. M. Darley, *The Unresponsive Bystander: Why Doesn't He Help?* Englewood Cliffs, N.J.: Prentice Hall, 1970.

Latané, B., and S. Wolf, "The Social Impact of Majorities and Minorities," *Psychological Review*, No. 88, 1981, pp. 438–453.

Lazarsfeld, P., D. Berelson, and H. Gaudet, *The People's Choice: How the Voter Makes Up His Mind in a Presidential Campaign*, New York: Duell, Sloan, and Pearce, 1948.

Lazarus, R. S., *Emotion and Adaptation*, New York: Oxford University Press, 1991.

Leventhal, H., "Findings and Theory in the Study of Fear Communications," in L. Berkowitz, ed., *Advances in Experimental Social Psychology*, Vol. 5, New York: Academic Press, 1970.

Levine, R. A., and D. T. Campbell, *Ethnocentrism: Theories of Conflict, Ethnic Attitudes and Group Behavior*, New York: Wiley, 1972.

Lichtenstein, S., and B. Fischhoff, "Do Those Who Know More Also Know More About How Much They Know?" *Organizational Behavior and Human Performance*, No. 20, 1977, pp. 159–183.

Liebert, R., and J. Sprafkin, *The Early Window: Effects of Television on Children and Youth*, 3rd edition, New York: Pergamon Press, 1988.

Likert, R., "A Technique for the Measurement of Attitudes," *Archives of Psychology*, No. 140, 1932.

Linville, P. W., G. W. Fischer, and P. Salovey, "Perceived Distributions of Characteristics of In-Group and Out-Group Members: Empirical Evidence and a Computer Simulation," *Journal of Personality and Social Psychology*, No. 57, 1989, pp. 165–188.

Lippmann, W., *Public Opinion*, New York: Harcourt-Brace, 1922.

Locke, E. A., and G. P. Latham, *A Theory of Goal Setting and Task Performance*, Englewood Cliffs, N.J.: Prentice Hall, 1990.

Loomes, G., and R. Sugden, "Regret Theory: An Alternative Theory of Rational Choice Under Uncertainty," *Economic Journal*, No. 92, 1982, pp. 805–824.

———, "A Rationale for Preference Reversal," *American Economic Review*, No. 73, 1983, pp. 428–432.

_____, "Some Implications of a More General Form of Regret Theory," *Journal of Economic Theory*, No. 41, 1987, pp. 270–287.

Maas, A., and L. Acuri, "Language and Stereotyping," in C. N. Macrae, C. Stangor, and M. Hewstone, eds., *Stereotypes and Stereotyping*, New York: Guilford, 1996.

Macklin, M., and L. Carlson, eds., *Advertising to Children*, Thousand Oaks, Calif.: Sage Publications, 1999.

Marks, G., and N. Miller, "Ten Years of Research on the False Consensus Effect: An Empirical and Theoretical Review," *Psychological Bulletin*, No. 102, 1987, pp. 72–90.

Markus, H., "Self-Schemata and Processing Information About the Self," *Journal of Personality and Social Psychology*, No. 35, 1977, pp. 63–78.

Marwell, G., and D. R. Schmitt, "Dimensions of Compliance-Gaining Behavior: An Empirical Analysis," *Sociometry*, No. 30, 1967, pp. 350–364.

Maslach, C., J. Stapp, and R. Santee, "Individuation: Concept Analysis and Assessment," *Journal of Personality and Social Psychology*, No. 49, 1985, pp. 729–738.

Maslow, A. (1943). "A Theory of Human Motivation," *Psychological Review*, Vol. 50, 1943, pp. 370–396.

McClelland, D. C., and D. H. Burnham, "Power Is the Great Motivator," *Harvard Business Review*, Vol. 54, No. 2, 1976, pp. 100–110.

McGuire, W., and D. Papageorgis, "Effectiveness of Forewarning in Developing Resistance to Persuasion," *Public Opinion Quarterly*, No. 26, 1962, pp. 24–34.

McGuire, W. J., "Personality and Attitude Change: An Information Processing Theory," in A. G. Greenwald, T. C. Brock, and T. M. Ostrom, eds., *Psychological Foundations of Attitudes*, San Diego, Calif.: Academic Press, 1968, pp. 171–196.

_____, "Theoretical Foundations of Campaigns," in R. E. Rice and C. K. Atkin, eds., *Public Communication Campaigns*, 2nd edition, Newbury Park, Calif.: Sage Publications, 1989, pp. 43–65.

McKillip, J., and S. L. Reidel, "External Validity of Matching on Physical Attractiveness for Same and Opposite Sex Couples," *Journal of Applied Social Psychology*, No. 13, 1983, pp. 328–337.

McLaughlin, M. L., M. J. Cody, and C. S. Robey, "Situational Influences of the Selection of Strategies to Resist Compliance-Gaining Attempts," *Human Communication Research*, No. 7, 1980, pp. 14–36.

Merton, R. K., "The Self-Fulfilling Prophecy," *The Antioch Review*, No. 8, 1948, pp. 193–210.

Michaels, J. W., J. M. Blommel, R. M. Brocato, R. A. Linkous, and J. S. Rowe, "Social Facilitation and Inhibition in a Natural Setting," *Replications in Social Psychology*, No. 2, 1982, pp. 21–24.

Milgram, S., "Behavioral Study of Obedience," *Journal of Abnormal and Social Psychology*, Vol. 67, 1963, pp. 371–378.

Miller, N., and J. Dollard, *Social Learning and Imitation*, New Haven, Conn.: Yale University Press, 1941.

Miller, N., and D. T. Campbell, "Recency and Primacy in Persuasion as a Function of the Timing of Speeches and Measurements," *Journal of Abnormal and Social Psychology*, No. 59, 1959, pp. 1–9.

Miller, R. L., "Mere Exposure, Psychological Reactance and Attitude Change," *Journal of Abnormal and Social Psychology*, No. 59, 1976, pp. 1–9.

Mintzberg, H., *Power In and Around Organisations*, Engelwood Cliffs, N.J.: Prentice Hall, 1983.

Moscovici, S., "The Phenomenon of Social Representations," in R. M. Farr and S. Moscovici, eds., *Social Representations*, Cambridge, UK: Cambridge University Press, 1984.

_____, "Three Concepts: Minority, Conflict and Behavioral Style," in S. Moscovici, A. Mucchi-Faina, and A. Maass, eds., *Minority Influence*, Chicago: Nelson-Hall, 1994, pp. 233–251.

Moscovici, S., and M. Hewstone, "Social Representations and Social Explanations: From the 'Naïve' to the 'Amateur' Scientist," in M. Hewstone, ed., *Attribution Theory: Social and Functional Extensions*, Oxford, UK: Blackwell Publishing, 1983.

Moscovici, S., and C. Nemeth, "Minority Influence," in C. Nemeth, ed., *Social Psychology: Classic and Contemporary Integrations* Chicago: Rand McNally, 1974, pp. 217–249.

Moscovici, S., and M. Zavalloni, "The Group as a Polarizer of Attitudes," *Journal of Personality and Social Psychology*, No. 12, 1969, pp. 125–135.

Myers, D. G., and G. D. Bishop, "Discussion Effects on Racial Attitudes," *Science*, No. 169, 1970, pp. 778–779.

Nisbett, R., and L. Ross, *Human Inference: Strategies and Shortcomings of Social Judgment*, Englewood Cliffs, N.J.: Prentice Hall, 1980.

Nisbett, R. E., H. Zukier, and R. Lemley, "The Dilution Effect: Nondiagnostic Information Weakens the Implications of Diagnostic Information," *Cognitive Psychology*, No. 13, 1981, pp. 248–277.

Ogilvy, D., *Ogilvy on Advertising*, New York: Vintage Books, 1987.

Osgood, C., G. Suci, P. Tannenbaum, *The Measurement of Meaning*, Urbana, Ill.: University of Illinois Press, 1957.

Papageorgis, D., "Warning and Persuasion," *Psychological Bulletin*, No. 70, 1968, pp. 271–282.

Papageorgis, D., and W. J. McGuire, "The Generality of Immunity to Persuasion Produced by Pre-Exposure to Weakened Counterarguments," *Journal of Abnormal and Social Psychology*, No. 62, 1961, pp. 475–481.

Payne, J. W., "Contingent Decision Behavior," *Psychological Bulletin*, No. 80, 1982, pp. 439–453.

Pennington, N., and R. Hastie, "Evidence Evaluation in Complex Decision Making," *Journal of Personality and Social Psychology*, No. 51, 1986, pp. 242–258.

_____, "Explanation-Based Decision Making: The Effects of Memory Structure on Judgment," *Journal of Experimental Psychology: Learning, Memory, and Cognition*, No. 14, 1988, pp. 521–533.

_____, "Explaining the Evidence: Tests of the Story Model for Juror Decision Making," *Journal of Personality and Social Psychology*, No. 62, 1992, pp. 189–206.

Petri, H., *Motivation: Theory, Research and Application,* 3rd edition, Belmont, Calif.: Wadsworth, 1991.

Pettigrew, T. F., "The Ultimate Attribution Error: Extending Allport's Cognitive Analysis of Prejudice," *Personality and Social Psychology Bulletin*, No. 5, 1979, pp. 461–476.

Petty, R., and J. Cacioppo, "Forewarning, Cognitive Responding, and Resistance to Persuasion," *Journal of Personality and Social Psychology*, No. 35, 1977, pp. 645–655.

_____, "The Effect of Issue Involvement on Responses to Argument Quantity and Quality: Central and Peripheral Routes to Persuasion," *Journal of Personality and Social Psychology*, No. 46, 1984, pp. 69–81.

Pfeffer, J., *Managing with Power: Politics and Influence in Organizations*, Boston: Harvard Business School Press, 1992.

Phillips, D. P., "The Impact of Mass Media Violence on U.S. Homicides," *American Sociological Review*, No. 48, 1983, pp. 560–568.

_____, "Natural Experiments on the Effects of Mass Media Violence on Fatal Aggression: Strengths and Weaknesses of a New Approach," in L. Berkowitz, ed., *Advances in Experimental Social Psychology*, Vol. 19, 1986, pp. 207–250.

Pratkanis, A., and E. Aronson, *The Age of Propaganda*, New York: Freeman & Co., 2000.

Prentice, D. A., and D. T. Miller, "Pluralistic Ignorance and Alcohol Use on Campus: Some Consequences of Misperceiving the Social Norm," *Journal of Personality and Social Psychology*, No. 64, 1993, pp. 243–256.

Pruitt, D. G., "Choice Shifts in Group Discussion: An Introductory Review," *Journal of Personality and Social Psychology*, Vol. 20, No. 3, 1971, pp. 339–360.

Quattrone, G. A., "On the Perception of a Group's Variability," in S. Worchel and W. G. Austin, eds., *Psychology of Intergroup Relations*, 2nd edition, Chicago: Nelson-Hall, 1986.

Quattrone, G. A., and A. Tversky, "Contrasting Rational and Psychological Analyses of Political Choice," *American Political Science Review*, No. 82, 1988, pp. 719–736.

Rogers, E., and F. Shoemaker, *Communication of Innovations: A Cross-Cultural Approach*, New York: Free Press, 1971.

Rosnow, R., "Whatever Happened to the 'Law of Primacy'," *Journal of Communication*, No. 16, 1966, pp. 10–31.

Rosnow, R., and E. Robinson, *Experiments in Persuasion*, New York: Academic Press, 1967.

Ross, L., and C. Anderson, "Shortcomings in Attribution Processes: On the Origins and Maintenance of Erroneous Social Judgments," in D. Kahneman, P. Slovic, and A. Tversky, eds., *Judgment Under Uncertainty: Heuristics and Biases*, New York: Cambridge University Press, 1982.

Ross, L., T. M. Amabile, and J. L. Steinmetz, "Social Roles, Social Control and Biases in Social Perception," *Journal of Personality and Social Psychology*, No. 35, 1977, pp. 485–494.

Ross, L., M. R. Lepper, and M. Hubbard, "Perseverance in Self-Perception and Social Perception: Biased Attributional Processes in the Debriefing Paradigm," *Journal of Personality and Social Psychology*, No. 32, 1975, pp. 880–892.

Rubin, J., and N. Friedland, "Theater of Terror," *Psychology Today*, Vol. 20, No. 3, 1986, pp. 18–28.

Russell, G., and R. L. Arms, "Toward a Social Psychological Profile of Would-Be Rioters," *Aggressive Behavior*, No. 24, 1998, pp. 219–226.

Russell, G., and A. Mustonen, "Peacemakers: Those Who Would Intervene to Quell a Sports Riot," *Personality and Individual Differences*, No. 24, 1998, pp. 335–339.

Russell, G., R. Arms, and A. Mustonen, "When Cooler Heads Prevail: Peacemakers in a Sports Riot," *Scandinavian Journal of Psychology*, No. 40, 1999, pp. 153–156.

Saunders G., ed., *Samizdat: Voices of the Soviet Opposition*, New York: Pathfinder Press, 2001.

Sawyer, A. G., "Repetition, Cognitive Responses and Persuasion," in R. E. Petty, T. M. Ostrom, and T. C. Brock, eds., *Cognitive Responses In Persuasion*, Hillsdale, N.J.: Lawrence Erlbaum Associates, 1981, pp. 237–261.

Schachter, S., "The Interaction of Cognitive and Physiological Determinants of Emotional State," in L. Berkowitz, ed., *Advances in Experimental Social Psychology*, Vol. 1, New York: Academic Press, 1964, pp. 49–80.

Schachter, S., and J. E. Singer, "Cognitive, Social and Physiological Determinants of Emotional States," *Psychological Review*, No. 69, 1962, pp. 379–399.

Schafer, M., and S. Crichlow, "Antecedents of Groupthink: A Quantitative Study," *Journal of Conflict Resolution*, No. 40, 1996, pp. 415–435.

Schul, Y., "When Warning Succeeds: The Effect of Warning on Success of Ignoring Invalid Information," *Journal of Experimental Social Psychology*, No. 29, 1993, pp. 42–62.

Schul, Y., and E. Burnstein, "When Discounting Fails: Conditions Under Which Individuals Use Discredited Information in Making a Judgment," *Journal of Personality and Social Psychology*, No. 49, 1985, pp. 894–903.

Schul, Y., E. Burnstein, and A. Bardi, "Dealing with Deceptions That Are Difficult to Detect: Encoding and Judgment as a Function of Preparing to Receive Invalid Information," *Journal of Experimental Social Psychology*, No. 32, 1996, pp. 228–253.

Schul, Y., E. Burnstein, and J. Martinez, "The Informational Basis of Social Judgments: Under What Conditions Are Inconsistent Trait Descriptions Processed as Easily as Consistent Ones?" *European Journal of Social Psychology*, No. 13, 1983, pp. 143–151.

Schul, Y., and D. Mazursky, "Conditions Facilitating Successful Discounting in Consumer Decision-Making," *Journal of Consumer Research*, No. 16, 1990, pp. 442–451.

Sherif, C. W., M. Sherif, and R. E. Nebergall, *Attitude and Attitude Change: The Social Judgment-Involvement Approach*, Philadelphia, Pa.: W. B. Saunders, 1965.

Sherif, M., *In Common Predicament: Social Psychology of Intergroup Conflict and Cooperation*, Boston: Houghton Mifflin, 1966.

Sherif, M., and C. W. Sherif, "Attitudes as the Individual's Own Categories: The Social-Judgment Approach to Attitude and Attitude Change," in C. W. Sherif and M. Sherif, eds., *Attitude, Ego-Involvement and Change*, New York: Wiley, 1967, pp. 105–139.

Sherif, M., D. Taub, and C. I. Hovland, "Assimilation and Contrast Effects of Anchoring Stimuli on Judgments," *Journal of Experimental Psychology*, No. 55, 1958, pp. 150–155.

Simon, H. A., "Rational Choice and the Structure of the Environment," *Psychological Review*, No. 63, 1956, pp. 129–138.

Slovic, P., "Perception of Risk," *Science*, No. 236, 1987, pp. 280–285.

Slovic, P., and B. Fischhoff, "On the Psychology of Experimental Surprises," *Journal of Experimental Psychology: Human Perception and Performance*, No. 3, 1977, pp. 544–551.

Snyder, M., and E. Jones, "Attitude Attribution When Behavior Is Constrained," *Journal of Experimental Social Psychology*, No. 10, 1974, pp. 585–600.

Snyder, M., and N. Cantor, "Testing Hypotheses About Other People: The Use of Historical Knowledge," *Journal of Experimental Social Psychology*, No. 15, 1979, pp. 330–342.

Sproule, J., *Channels of Propaganda*, Bloomington, Ind.: Edinfo Press, 1994.

Staub, E., *The Roots of Evil: The Origins of Genocide and Other Group Violence*, New York: Cambridge University Press, 1989.

Steblay, N. M., "Helping Behavior in Rural and Urban Environments: A Meta-Analysis," *Psychological Bulletin*, No. 102, 1987, pp. 346–356.

Stiff, J. B., *Persuasive Communication*, New York: Guilford, 1994.

Swann, W., B. Pelham, and T. Chidester, "Change Through Paradox: Using Self-Verification to Alter Beliefs," *Journal of Personality and Social Psychology*, No. 54, 1988, pp. 268–273.

Swann, W., and R. Ely, "A Battle of Wills: Self-Verification Versus Behavioral Confirmation," *Journal of Personality and Social Psychology*, No. 46, 1984, pp. 1287–1302.

Tajfel, H., "Experiments in Intergroup Discrimination," *Scientific American*, No. 223, 1970, pp. 96–102.

_____, *Social Identity and Intergroup Relations*, Cambridge, UK: Cambridge University Press, 1982.

Tajfel, H., and J. C. Turner, "The Social Identity Theory of Inter-Group Behavior," in S. Worchel and L. W. Austin, eds., *Psychology of Intergroup Relations*, Chicago: Nelson-Hall, 1986.

Tanford, S., and S. Penrod, "Social Influence Model: A Formal Integration of Research on Majority and Minority Influence Processes," *Psychological Bulletin*, No. 95, 1984, pp. 189–225.

Taylor, S. E., and S. T. Fiske, "Point of View and Perception of Causality," *Journal of Personality and Social Psychology*, No. 32, 1975, pp. 439–445.

Taylor, S. E., and J. H. Koivumaki, "The Perception of Self and Others: Acquaintanceship, Affect and Actor-Observer Differences," *Journal of Personality and Social Psychology*, No. 33, 1976, pp. 403–408.

Tesser, A., "Towards a Self-Evaluative Maintenance Model of Social Behavior," in L. Berkowitz, ed., *Advances in Experimental Social Psychology*, Vol. 21, Orlando, Fla.: Academic Press, 1988, pp. 181–227.

Tesser, A., L. Martin, and M. Mendolia, "The Impact of Thought on Attitude Extremity and Attitude-Behavior Consistency," in R. E. Petty and J. A. Krosnick, eds., *Attitude Strength: Antecedents and Consequences*, Hillsdale, N.J.: Lawrence Erlbaum Associates, 1995, pp. 73–92.

Tetlock, P. E., and J. Kim, "Accountability and Judgment in a Personality Prediction Task," *Journal of Personality and Social Psychology: Attitudes and Social Cognition,* No. 52, 1987, pp. 700–709.

Thaler, R., "Towards a Positive Theory of Consumer Choice," *Journal of Economic Behavior and Organization*, No. 1, 1980, pp. 39–60.

Thurstone, L., *The Measurement of Attitudes*, Chicago: University of Chicago Press, 1929.

Tversky, A., and D. Kahneman, "The Belief in the Law of Small Numbers," *Psychological Bulletin*, No. 76, 1971, pp. 105–110.

_____, "Judgment Under Uncertainty: Heuristics and Biases," *Science*, No. 185, 1974, pp. 1124–1130.

_____, "The Framing of Decisions and Psychology of Choice," *Science*, No. 211, 1981, pp. 453–458.

U.S. Special Operations Command, *Post-Operational Analysis: Iraqi PSYOP During DESERT SHIELD/STORM*, 1992.

Vallone, R. P., L. Ross, and M. R. Lepper, "The Hostile Media Phenomenon: Biased Perception and Perceptions of Media Bias in Coverage of the Beirut Massacre," *Journal of Personality and Social Psychology*, No. 49, 1985, pp. 577–585.

Varela, J., *Psychological Solutions to Social Problems: An Introduction to Social Technology*, New York: Academic Press, 1971.

Walster, E., G. W. Walster, and E. Berscheid, *Equity: Theory and Research*, Boston: Allyn and Bacon, 1978.

Walton, D., *Appeal to Expert Opinion: Arguments from Authority*, University Park, Pa.: Penn State University Press, 1997.

Watzlawick, P., J. Weakland, and R. Fisch, *Change: Principles of Problem Formation and Problem Resolution*, New York: Norton, 1971.

White, P. H., and S. G. Harkins, "Race of Source Effects in the Elaboration Likelihood Model," *Journal of Personality and Social Psychology*, No. 67, 1994, pp. 790–807.

Wickland, R., and J. Brehm, *Perspectives on Cognitive Dissonance*, New York: Halsted Press, 1976.

Witte, K., "Putting the Fear Back into Fear Appeals: The Extended Parallel Process Model," *Communication Monographs*, No. 59, 1992, pp. 329–349.

_____, "Fear Control and Danger Control: A Test of the Extended Parallel Process Model," *Communications Monographs*, Vol. 61, No. 2, 1994, pp. 113–134.

Zajonc, R. B., "Attitudinal Effects of Mere Exposure," *Journal of Personality and Social Psychology*, No. 9, Monograph Supplement No. 2, Part 2, 1968.

Zanot, E. J., J. D. Pincus, and E. J. Lamp, "Public Perceptions of Subliminal Advertising," *Journal of Advertising*, Vol. 12, No. 1, 1983, pp. 39–45.

Zimbardo, P. G., "The Human Choice: Individuation, Reason, and Order Versus Deindividuation, Impulse, and Chaos," *Nebraska Symposium on Motivation*, No. 17, 1969, pp. 237–307.

_____, "On 'Obedience to Authority'," *American Psychologist*, No. 29, No. 7, 1974, pp. 566–567.

Zuckerman, M., and R. E. Driver, "Telling Lies: Verbal and Nonverbal Correlates of Deception," in A. W. Siegman and S. Feldstein, eds., *Multi-Channel Integrations of Non-Verbal Behavior*, Hillsdale, N.J.: Erlbaum, 1985, pp. 129–147.

Zuckerman, M., B. M. Depaulo, and R. Rosenthal, "Verbal and Non-Verbal Communication of Deception," in L. Berkowitz, ed., *Advances in Experimental and Social Psychology*, Vol. 14, New York: Academic Press, 1981, pp. 1–59.